WAR AT SEA
IN THE
IRONCLAD AGE

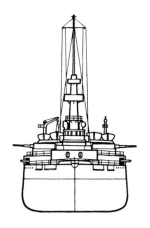

WAR AT SEA
IN THE
IRONCLAD AGE

Richard Hill

General Editor: John Keegan

CASSELL&CO

First published in Great Britain 2000
by Cassell, Wellington House, 125 Strand, London
WC2R 0BB

British Library Cataloguing-in-publication Data
ISBN: 0-304-35273-X

Cartography and picture research: Arcadia Editions
Design: Martin Hendry
Picture Research: Elaine Willis

Typeset in Monotype Sabon
Printed in Italy by Printer Trento S.r.l.

ACKNOWLEDGEMENTS

This book would not have been possible without the help of a large number of people. I must acknowledge a debt to Andrew Lambert for his analysis of Victorian naval strategy, to John Winton for his knowledge of life and education in the navies of the period and to David K. Brown for his masterly analysis of the material developments. These were the three authorities I chose ten years ago to cover the period in *The Oxford Illustrated History of the Royal Navy* of which I was General Editor; they amply showed their capacity there, and this work owes much to each of them.

I received help from many archivists and librarians up and down the country. At the Royal Naval Museum, Portsmouth, Allison Wareham found, both in the newly installed section of the Admiralty Library and in the King Alfred Library, all kinds of intriguing works of the period and later, that bore on the subject. Jenny Wraight at the Naval Historical Branch in London similarly provided some rare books unobtainable elsewhere. The National Maritime Museum, in particular its Historic Photographs and Ship Plans Section, was of great help in locating and sorting the masses of photographic material that are available. The British Naval Attachés at Rome and Moscow each supplied one of those dates that are so maddeningly elusive to complete the potted biographies.

At the publishers my thanks are due to Nicholas Chapman for setting the project off and for his valuable suggestions on a first reading of the text; to Caroline Knight for her help and cheerful encouragement; to Penny Gardiner for seeing the book through to completion; and to Elaine Willis for expert picture research. It is also very right and proper to thank John Keegan for thinking of me as an author even though he knew it was a new topic for me, and Malcolm Swanston who has so amply justified his high reputation in producing the outstanding maps and plans.

Finally, I have as always to thank my wife Patricia for her kindness and forbearance during the time when I was not only finishing this work, but unexpectedly taking on another major project for publication in the same year. It has been tough going and I hope the results justify it. As always, all the mistakes are mine.

RICHARD HILL
Bishop's Waltham

The Japanese battleship Mikasa *in dry dock during the early 1900s.*

CONTENTS

KEY TO MAPS

Military movements

- attack
- retreat
- battle

Ships

- gunboat
- turret-ship
- centre-battery ship
- floating battery
- mortar vessel
- paddle gunboat
- line-of-battle ship

Geographical symbols

- urban area
- road
- river
- seasonal river
- canal
- border
- railroads

MAP LIST

CHRONOLOGY

1855 War against Russia.
May Sea of Azov operations.
Aug Reduction of Sweaborg.
Oct Reduction of Kinburn, with first use of armoured vessels by the French.

1856
Jan Threat of Sweaborg treatment to Kronstadt influences Russians to accept peace terms.
March Treaty of Paris. Privateering abolished.
April Spithead Review.
Oct Outbreak of Second China War.

1857
Feb–May Anti-piracy operations in the Hong Kong area.
June Battle of Fatshan Creek.
Aug Royal Navy ships arrive in Indian waters to assist in quelling the Mutiny; naval brigades formed.
Dec Canton occupied by British and French forces.

1858
March French ironclad *Gloire* laid down.
May Anglo-French force captures Taku forts.
June Treaty of Tientsin.
July Funds allocated for *Warrior*, first British ironclad.

1859
Jan British Royal Commission on Naval Manning reports.
May *Warrior* laid down.
June Further difficulties with China: British attack on the Peiho forts fails.
Aug Naval Reserve authorized.

1860
March Local operations in New Zealand.
April New leave regulations in the Royal Navy.
Aug British/French force of 20,000 captures Taku forts.
Institution of Naval Architects founded.
Royal Commission on Naval Defence emphasizes security of bases.

1861
April Outbreak of American Civil War.
May *Warrior* in service.
Truce in New Zealand.
Nov The *Trent* incident: resentment at Union boarding of British mail steamer.

1862
March Battle of Hampton Roads (*Virginia* and *Monitor*), first major action between ironclad warships.
April Farragut captures New Orleans.
Aug Confederate commerce-raider *Alabama* begins two-year cruise.
Oct British support for Chinese Imperial Government ends.

1863
Jan–Apr Unsuccessful Union assaults on Charleston.
May Further outbreak of war in New Zealand.
July Reed becomes Chief Constructor to the Royal Navy.
July Surrender of Vicksburg: Mississippi cleared.
Aug Bombardment of Kagoshima: accidents with breech-loaders lead to retention of muzzle-loaders in Royal Navy.

1864
May Danish force defeats Austro-Prussians off the Elbe: ineffective owing to Prussian land victories.
June CSS *Alabama* sunk by USS *Kearsarge* off Cherbourg.
USS *Housatonic* and CSS *Albemarle* sunk by spar torpedoes.
Aug Farragut enters Mobile Bay.
Sept Royal Navy's School of Naval Architecture founded.
Strait of Shimonoseki, Japan, forced by Franco/Dutch/

American/British naval units.

1865

Jan — Capture of Fort Fisher by Union forces.
Bellerophon, first centre-battery ship, in service.

April — Lee surrenders to Grant.

May — American Civil War ends.

1866

June — Prussia and Italy at war with Austria. Italians defeated on land at Custozza, Austrians at Sadowa.

July — Battle of Lissa: tactical victory for Austrian fleet under Tegetthoff; Italian battleship sunk by ram.
Captain and *Monarch*, rival British fully-rigged turret-ships, laid down.

1867 — John Colomb disputes Britain's base protection strategy.

1868

Jan — Naval brigade takes part in British Abyssinian expedition.

1869 — Grivel publishes *De la Guerre Maritime*, forerunner of the *Jeune École*.

1870

July — Franco-Prussian War.
French naval blockade of Hamburg ineffective owing to rapid

Prussian victories on land.

Sept — Loss of the *Captain* in an Atlantic gale.

1871

Devastation, first mastless battleship, in service.
Many smaller 'Monitor' types, for harbour defence, launched for British and other navies.
Admiralty committee recommends introduction of compound engines.

1872

Commander 'Jacky' Fisher appointed Torpedo Instructor.
Britain and France acquire Whitehead torpedo technology.

Sept — *Vanguard* sunk by *Iron Duke* in ramming incident.

1873

April — Incursion by Ashanti forces into Fanti territory, Gold Coast; initial holding operations by Naval and Marine forces alone.

Oct — British army expedition under Wolseley lands on Gold Coast; naval brigade accompanies it.

1874

Feb — Battle of Amoaful. British forces withdraw to Gold Coast after occupying Kumasi.

1875

Rigged turret-ships continue to be built as front-line strength in the Royal Navy, but masts and sails

are seen as increasingly irrelevant in action; only French, Russian and Italian navies are serious contenders and none approach British numbers.

1876

Lightning, torpedo boat, built for Royal Navy by Thornycroft.
Hertz Horn mine developed.

May — British cruiser *Shah* fights drawn battle with rebel Peruvian turret-ship *Huascar*.

June — Further low-intensity operations and gunboat diplomacy on West African coast.

1878

Jan — Passage of Dardanelles by Mediterranean Fleet exerts deterrent pressure on Russia to solve the Eastern Question.

May — First production of Gilbert and Sullivan's *HMS Pinafore*.

Aug — Congress of Berlin: colonial expansion by all European powers sanctioned.

1879

Jan — Muzzle-loading gun explosion in *Thunderer* leads to slow re-introduction of breech-loading guns in Royal Navy.

March — Outbreak of the *Guerra del Pacifico* between Chile and Peru/Bolivia.

May	Weak Chilean force defeated off Iquique.	Feb	Baker Pasha's force defeated by Dervishes; British force landed on Egypt's Red Sea coast, supported by naval brigade, and defeats Osman Digna.		in France, and attempts to put the *Jeune École* into practice with concentration on light craft and cancellation of battleship programmes.
Oct	Battle of Angamos Point: Peruvian *Huascar* surrenders to superior Chilean force. Chile gains command of the sea.				
1880					William White becomes Director of Naval Construction in Britain.
Nov	Outbreak of First Boer War.	Oct	British relief force under Wolseley proceeds up the Nile. US Naval War College founded. Royal Corps of Naval Constructors founded. French naval forces under Courbet establish control in Indo-China and Pescadores.		
1881				**1887**	Experimental submarines operating in France, Britain, USA. British Colonial Conference agrees to form a trade protection squadron for Australian and New Zealand waters.
Jan	Fall of Lima to Chilean forces. Colley's British force in South Africa supported by naval brigade; defeat at Laing's Nek.				
Feb	Colley defeated and killed at Majuba Hill.				
March	Transvaal achieves independence.	**1885**		**1888**	Accession of Kaiser Wilhelm II in Germany.
May	Arabi Pasha leads revolt in Egypt.	Jan	Naval brigade crosses the great bend in the Nile. Beresford in the *Safieh* proceeds up the Nile; Wilson's upriver journey too late to save Gordon.	Sept	Tryon's success with attacking force in annual fleet manoeuvres alarms British opinion.
1882				**1889**	Belleville water-tube boilers adopted for French Navy. First fitting of triple-expansion engines in British battleships. Institute of Marine Engineers founded. Revised Royal Navy signal book issued. British Naval Defence Act establishes Two Power Standard for naval strength.
July	Bombardment of Alexandria by British Mediterranean Fleet. Egyptians driven from fortified positions after stubborn resistance; Beresford in the *Condor* a hero; British troops land in force in the wake of the operation.	March	Pendjeh incident: overt British preparations for Kronstadt campaign deter Russia from further encroachment in Afghanistan. Further operations against Osman Digna in Eastern Sudan. Convoy rejected by British Admiralty in favour of patrol stations for the protection of trade.		
1883	Dervish activity increases in Sudan.				
Oct	Hicks Pasha's force defeated by Dervishes. French establish partial control of Madagascar.				
1884		**1886**		**1890**	Mahan publishes *The Influence of Sea Power upon History*.
Jan	Gordon departs for Khartoum.	Jan	Aube becomes Minister of Marine		

	Building of navies by all major powers begins sharp acceleration. All-steel armour now in general use.	May	Dewey defeats Spanish force in Manila Bay, Philippines; Cervera's force arrives in Santiago, Cuba.	Fisher–Selborne Scheme for officers' training in the Royal Navy initiated. Philip Watts appointed Director of Naval Construction in UK.

1891 Large (over 10,000-ton) battleships under construction or in service in British, Chinese, French, Italian, Japanese, Russian and US Navies.

July — Battle of Santiago: Spanish force under Cervera annihilated by superior US fleet.

1903 German naval building programme gathers pace and triggers British counter-building.

1892 Royal Navy orders Belleville boilers for large cruisers. Introduction of optical rangefinders.

Sept — Fashoda incident: British mobilization checks French ambitions in Africa.

1904

Feb — Japanese attack on Russian fleet in Port Arthur.

1899

July — Fisher, British C-in-C in the Mediterranean, initiates widespread reforms.

April — Russian sortie from Port Arthur ends in mining of *Petropavlovsk*; death of C-in-C Makarov.

1893 French colonial administration relinquished by Ministry of Marine.

June — *Victoria* sunk by *Camperdown* in manoeuvring incident; Tryon drowned.

Oct — Outbreak of Second Boer War; naval brigades sent to Ladysmith, to accompany Buller's relief force and Kimberley relief force.

May — Heavy Japanese fleet casualties due to mining.

June — Battle of the Yellow Sea. C-in-C Vitgeft killed; Russian fleet forced to return to Port Arthur.

1894

Aug — Sino-Japanese War breaks out.

1900 Naval brigades continue work in South Africa. Advances in gunnery initiated by Percy Scott gather pace.

Sept — Battle of the Yalu: Ito defeats Chinese fleet; subsequent capture by Japan of Port Arthur and Wei-hai-wei.

Sept — Royal Naval College at Osborne opened.

Oct — Russian Baltic squadron under Rodzhestvensky sails for Far East.

June — Boxer Rising in China; capture of Taku forts.

1905

1897 Tirpitz appointed to Reich Navy Office.

June — Diamond Jubilee Review at Spithead; debut of *Turbinia*.

Aug — Relief of Peking legations.

May — Battle of Tsushima: Rodzhestvensky's force annihilated by Japanese fleet under Togo.

1901 'Battle of the Boilers' (water v. fire-tube) for the Royal Navy (until 1904).

1898

Jan — Insurrection in Cuba supported by public opinion in USA.

Oct — *Dreadnought* laid down: end of the Ironclad Age.

1902 Corbett appointed to Royal Naval War College as lecturer.

Feb — USS *Maine* blown up in Havana harbour.

April — USA declares war on Spain.

Jan — Anglo-Japanese Treaty.

TECHNICAL AND STRATEGIC CONTEXT

FRENCH SAILORS MANNING an early torpedo boat. In the 1870s and 1880s the French Jeune École *set much store on challenging British naval supremacy with fast, light craft, but internal dissensions and technical shortcomings meant the strategy was never fully implemented.*

TECHNICAL AND STRATEGIC CONTEXT

I T WAS A GREAT TEMPTATION, when invited to write a book with this title, to submit a three and a half word draft that read: 'There wasn't much.'

As further research showed, this would have been not only inadequate but inaccurate. Navies, their associated arms and their natural adversaries on the shore were used in every way the state of the art allowed, at some time and in some place, during the fifty years we can call the Ironclad Age, that is from 1855 to 1905. It is true that the Royal Navy was scarcely involved in major combat operations during the period, but it would be the depth of insularity to suggest that because of that fact the sea warfare of the time should be

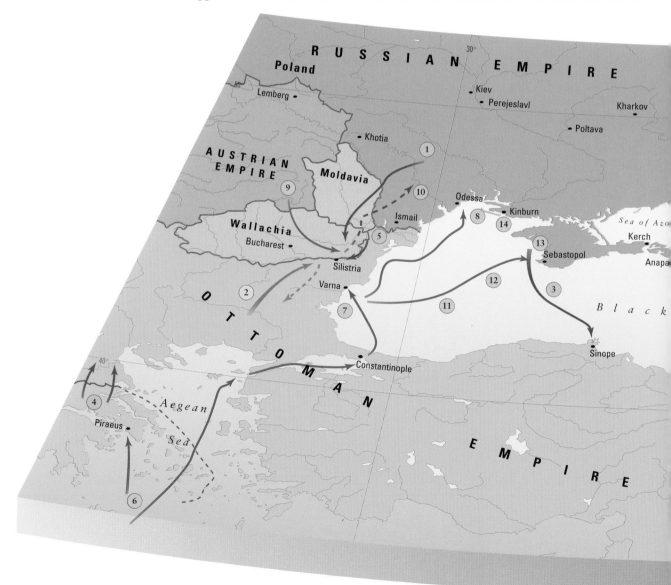

discounted. Operational exemplars among other naval powers were numerous, as subsequent chapters will show. If, meanwhile, the British Navy maintained a lofty stand-off, it was because it was powerful enough to safeguard the national interest without fighting; it was an exemplar too, but of deterrence not of major war-making.

The limits of the Ironclad Age are fairly easy to set. Its archetypal instrument of sea power, the fighting ship, had three chief characteristics: a metal-skinned hull, steam propulsion and a main armament of guns capable of firing exploding shells. It is only when all three characteristics are present that a fighting ship can properly be called an ironclad; and by that token, the first ironclads to be used in action were the French 'floating batteries' in the bombardment of the forts at Kinburn in 1855. Similarly, the end of the Age is relatively simple to

OVERLEAF: *A British battleship firing a salute in Spithead, 1886. Such conscious demonstrations of grandeur, discipline and military might were more common than battles between large-scale fleets, but this did not belittle the influence of sea power.*

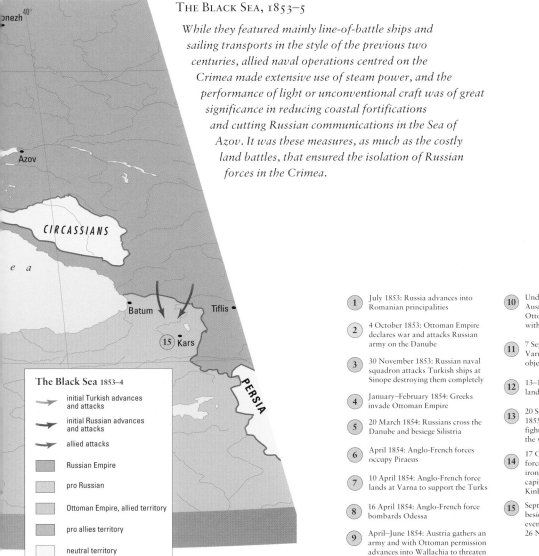

THE BLACK SEA, 1853–5

While they featured mainly line-of-battle ships and sailing transports in the style of the previous two centuries, allied naval operations centred on the Crimea made extensive use of steam power, and the performance of light or unconventional craft was of great significance in reducing coastal fortifications and cutting Russian communications in the Sea of Azov. It was these measures, as much as the costly land battles, that ensured the isolation of Russian forces in the Crimea.

The Black Sea 1853–4

→ initial Turkish advances and attacks

→ initial Russian advances and attacks

→ allied attacks

▮ Russian Empire

▮ pro Russian

▮ Ottoman Empire, allied territory

▮ pro allies territory

☐ neutral territory

1. July 1853: Russia advances into Romanian principalities

2. 4 October 1853: Ottoman Empire declares war and attacks Russian army on the Danube

3. 30 November 1853: Russian naval squadron attacks Turkish ships at Sinope destroying them completely

4. January–February 1854: Greeks invade Ottoman Empire

5. 20 March 1854: Russians cross the Danube and besiege Silistria

6. April 1854: Anglo-French forces occupy Piraeus

7. 10 April 1854: Anglo-French force lands at Varna to support the Turks

8. 16 April 1854: Anglo-French force bombards Odessa

9. April–June 1854: Austria gathers an army and with Ottoman permission advances into Wallachia to threaten the Russian forces

10. Under the combined threat of Austria, Britain, France and the Ottoman Empire, the Russian army withdraws

11. 7 September 1854: allied force leaves Varna in 150 ships, with the objective of occupying Sebastopol

12. 13–18 September 1854: allied force lands 30 miles north of Sebastopol

13. 20 September 1854 – 9 September 1855: allies besiege Sebastopol and fight several major land battles in the vicinity

14. 17 October 1855: Anglo-French force, including the first use of ironclads, bombards and forces capitulation of the Russian forts at Kinburn

15. September–November 1855: Kars is besieged by Russian army, eventually surrendering on 26 November

define, for the 'Dreadnought' all-big-gun class of 1905 was a step change in the design of fighting ships, and the battle fleets that fought ten years later were quite different from ironclads even though they had evolved from them. Moreover, new dimensions were being introduced at the beginning of the twentieth century by the submarine and the aircraft; sea warfare was never going to be the same again.

If then it is easy to place the Ironclad Age within precise limits of time, is there similarly a strategic context that corresponds with it? It is tempting to say that there is. Clausewitz published *On War* in the 1820s and Darwin *The Origin of Species* in 1859. These two works informed the whole of strategy and indeed politics in the next half-century. The German's view of war as an instrument of policy serving the interests of, and conducted by, whole nations rather than professional forces acting on behalf of monarchs, together with the Briton's doctrine of the survival of the fittest, were instrumental in forging a power-based set of criteria for national conduct. The instruments and management of war were part of the power base.

These ideas were also influential in the development of nation-states where previously there had been loose associations of weak sub-national units, as in Germany and Italy; and in the acquisition of overseas empires. The pattern for the latter had been set by Britain – though significantly, it was not until 1877, twenty years after the Indian Mutiny, that Victoria was proclaimed Queen Empress. Before that, declared empires had been aplenty but they had been European; overseas colonies were possessions. Now began a rush for Empire overseas that is, in the public perception nowadays, one of the least attractive aspects of the rest of the nineteenth century. It could not have taken place without sea power.

Sea power in its broadest sense included the instruments of commerce as well as those of war. Merchant ships, many of them still propelled principally by sail, multiplied, and trade increased enormously. The stakes of the Western world – above all Britain, which had a merchant fleet four times as large as any other – in this trade were extremely high and the wars that did occur tended to affect it only locally. Again, the deterrent effect of the Royal Navy should not be underestimated; but that is to some extent a judgement of hindsight. At the time, there was a widespread belief that trade protected itself.

The shattering of this belief, above all in the First World War, was one of the strategic changes that occurred as the Ironclad Age came to an end. There were others: the increasing dominance of firepower; the enormous increase in scale of military confrontation; and the inability of political leaders to control the forces, both populist and material, that they had to deal with. All help to define the strategic limit of the Age.

That then is the context, material and strategic, of the Ironclad Age. The rest of this book falls naturally within that context. It begins as it has to with a chapter on *matériel*, for it was material change that drove the development of navies and the ways in which they were employed, in peace, quasi-peace and war. The pace was rapid, often frenzied; sometimes the new technologies were scarcely tested before they were thrown into action, but more frequently they never saw action at all before they were in turn superseded. Competition within and among nations was fierce.

The next chapter deals with navies and their people; the changes of the half-century were profound, the workaday tarpaulins of 1855 transforming into almost idolized Jack Tars, and even more godlike officers, by 1905. This was not a phenomenon confined to Britain. It was aided by the concepts discussed in the third chapter; quite simply, sea power acquired a philosophical basis drawn from history which, however simplistic or flawed it might later appear, was found convincing at the time by the highest in many lands.

A fourth chapter is occupied by the American Civil War (1861–5). This was the largest-scale war at sea of the whole Ironclad Age, and by occurring near its beginning it offered 'firsts' in a multitude of fields. Two caveats must, however, be entered: it was a war that took place in some very special environments and therefore was not entirely typical; and it did not feature some of the characteristics of the Ironclad Age because they had not yet been developed.

The two final chapters span the remaining operations of the half-century, worldwide. They include not only operations of war, declared or undeclared, but of deterrence and colonial expansion. Thus there are examples of every kind of application of sea power from peaceable presence, through coercive deployments, expeditionary forays and minor encounters, to full-scale battle. All were operations that could not have occurred in the way they did without the use of steam or shellfire, though arguably some might have been able to do so without armour cladding except of the lightest sort. Though some were small in scale compared with the totality of naval force in the world at the time, they were in general seen as having marked, often decisive, significance in the conflicts in which they featured.

This perceived utility on a small scale was a powerful driver of the view that sea power would have exceptional influence on major conflict in the future: conflict which, in the Clausewitzian–Darwinian ethos, was regarded as certain to occur sooner or later. At the very end of the Ironclad Age the Russo-Japanese War, with its Wagnerian climax at the battle of Tsushima, seemed to bear out all the theories derived from the past and the predictions of the future.

Thus the Ironclad Age, on analysis, presents a satisfying whole in spite of its apparent fragmentation and frequently tentative progress. There were many mistakes and misconceived ideas, and it is hoped the book will give them due place. But the development of navies and of their use was a cardinal feature of the period, and its legacy was profound – not only in the conceptions of how wars might be fought, but in power balances and world polity, the effects of which are still with us today.

CHAPTER ONE

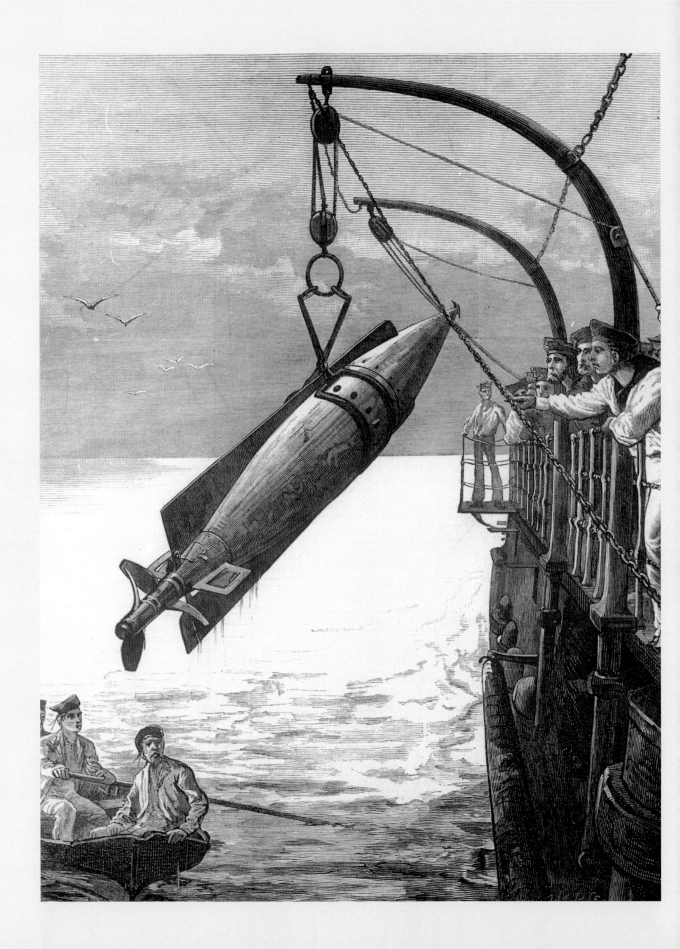

THE TECHNICAL BACKGROUND

An early Whitehead torpedo being hoisted after a trial run. The locomotive torpedo employed a system of depth and directional control invented by Robert Whitehead in the late 1860s, which in essentials continues today. Early models were, however, of very limited range and slow speed.

THE TECHNICAL BACKGROUND

THE IRONCLAD AGE, in the brief space of fifty years, saw the instruments of naval power progress – in three crucial areas – hull design and construction, propulsion and armament. Put briefly, it was a case of wood and sail and cannonballs to steel and steam and shells. These developments meant inevitably that any discussion of naval power took *matériel* as its starting point. It is said that armies equip and arm their troops, while navies man their armaments. That was never more true than in the Ironclad Age.

That is not to say that human and organizational factors were unimportant. The quality of people, their training, their resourcefulness and the way they were commanded, and how they were used both operationally and as forces in being, were all critical elements of effectiveness, and later chapters of this book will discuss them as fully as space allows. But the bedrock of the naval business was its *matériel*.

It is not surprising, then, that the literature of the period was awash with details of hull form and construction, armour, main and auxiliary machinery, guns and, later, torpedoes. Figures often acquired their own momentum and

Bombardment of Kinburn, 17 October 1855. The three French floating batteries are the low-lying vessels in the right centre of the picture. Their close approach to the Russian forts, made possible by their ability to withstand Russian counter-fire, is clearly indicated.

reputation. Competition both within nations and internationally was intense.

There were few enough wars to test the developments as they came along. The Royal Navy's numerical and, usually, technical superiority exercised a powerful deterrence, and such wars as did occur either did not concern Britain or were on a small scale and seldom involved the latest equipments against serious opposition. The more thoughtful designers and planners took careful note of such operational experience as there was, but much of their work was necessarily in the light airs of peace, with little of the wind of experience to drive them. The same went for all the major or emerging naval powers, though some – notably the French – did, as will be seen, reach out after developments that might reverse their position as the weaker naval power.

It must be recalled that the Ironclad Age at sea was essentially two-dimensional. That is to say, the surface warship was the only seagoing instrument of power. Its principal challengers were other surface warships or, if it chose to venture within their range, coastal forts. Towards the end of the period the third dimension, in the form of underwater and above-water weapon-carriers, was beginning to emerge, but for most of the period the surface was supreme. Thus this chapter, in its coverage of the rapid material development of the period, will concentrate on surface vessels under the headings of Hull, Propulsion and Armament, and only at the end give a hint of the coming of submarines and aircraft – both of which were so soon afterwards to change the face of sea warfare completely.

HULL DESIGN AND CONSTRUCTION

The first development in hull design of the Ironclad Age was, unsurprisingly, the cladding of warships with iron armour plate. This had first appeared in operational craft during the Russian War at the bombardment of Kinburn in 1855. Here, at the mouth of the Dnieper river, the French – stealing a march on the British who were developing similar craft – deployed three 'floating batteries' which, protected by iron armour, were able to move in close to the Russian shore works and take a major part in battering them to pieces. They did this at minimal cost in damage or casualties although repeatedly hit; the Russian projectiles, both shot and shell, bounced off or exploded harmlessly.

Soon afterwards the French Navy, urged by Napoleon III to challenge Britain's supremacy at sea, embarked on its first large-scale ironclad, the *Gloire*, designed by the great naval architect Dupuy de Lôme.

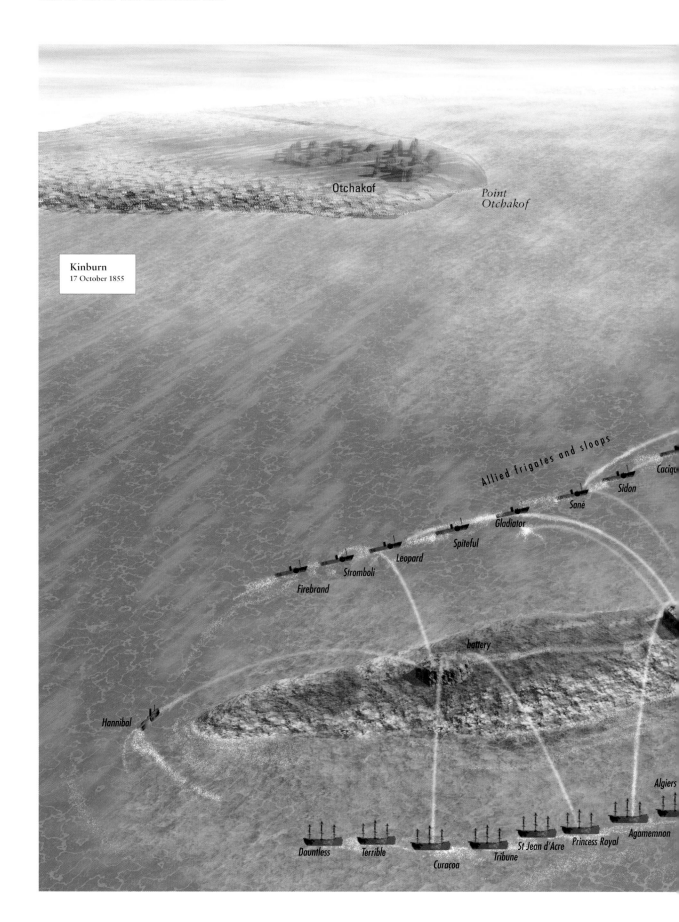

Otchakof

Point Otchakof

Kinburn
17 October 1855

Allied frigates and sloops

Caciqu

Sidon

Sané

Gladiator

Spiteful

Leopard

Stromboli

Firebrand

battery

Hannibal

Algiers

Dauntless

Terrible

Curaçoa

Tribune

St Jean d'Acre

Princess Royal

Agamemnon

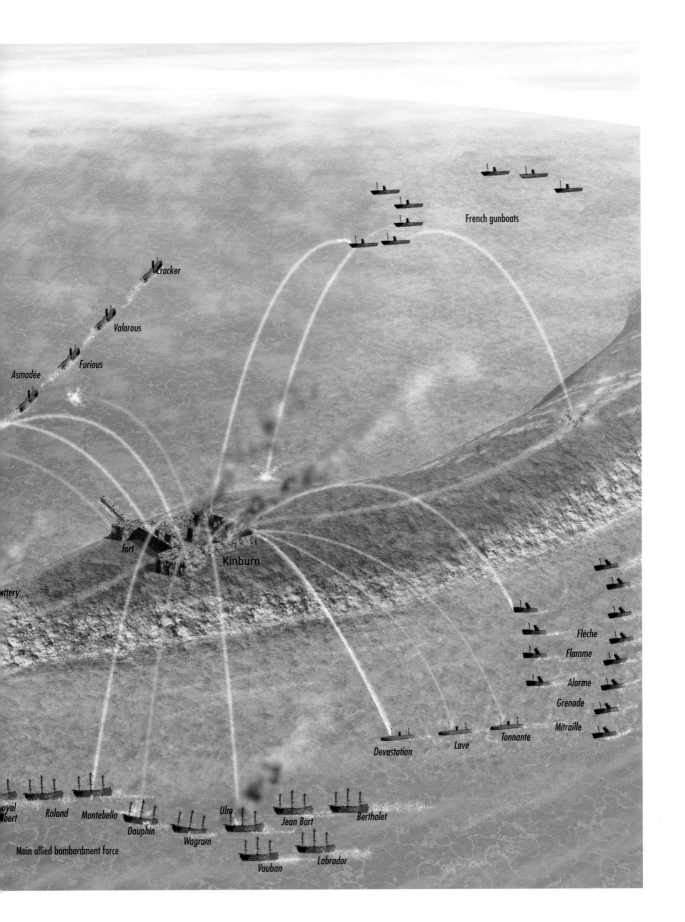

French gunboats

Cracker

Valorous

Furious

Asmodée

fort

Kinburn

ttery

Flèche

Flamme

Alarme

Grenade

Mitraille

Devastation

Lave

Tonnante

oyal
bert

Roland

Montebello

Ulm

Jean Bart

Bertholet

Dauphin

Wagram

Vauban

Labrador

Main allied bombardment force

HMS Warrior, *the first British ironclad, under construction. She was superior in fighting power to any other vessel in the world when she came into service in 1861, but towards the end of the decade was outclassed in her turn by rapid technical development. She never fired a shot in anger.*

But the British, encouraged by visionaries like John Scott Russell – who had already with Brunel produced the gigantic merchant ship *Great Eastern* – were already preparing something bigger and better: the *Warrior*.

This magnificent vessel, still happily afloat and superbly presented in the Heritage area at Portsmouth, England, was when completed in 1861 comfortably superior in fighting terms to anything else afloat. Iron-framed, her sides clad in 4-inch iron armour backed by two layers of teak, she was a monument to her chief designer Isaac Watts and her builders, Thames Ironworks at Blackwall. This showed the pattern of warship design and construction at this period: Watts was an Admiralty employee, designated the Chief Constructor, but the builders were a private firm and the engines and services were also from contractors. Later in the period the Royal Dockyards built a number of ships, including the biggest, but private yards continued to build the greater proportion of the navy's vessels.

The *Warrior* proved to be seaworthy, fast under power, and indeed sail too under her full three-masted rig, though she was none too handy under sail alone. She was followed through the early 1860s by a distinguished line of major warships

THE FRENCH *LA GLOIRE*

Designed by Dupuy de Lôme, La Gloire *was the first full-scale ocean-going ironclad, laid down in 1858. Built to the limits of available technology and industry in France, she was quickly outmatched by the larger, faster and more powerful British ironclad* Warrior.

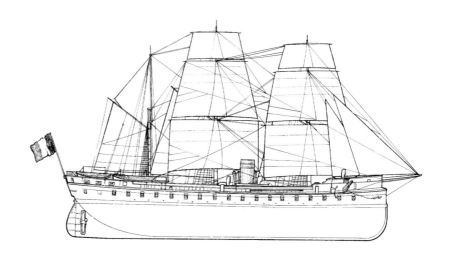

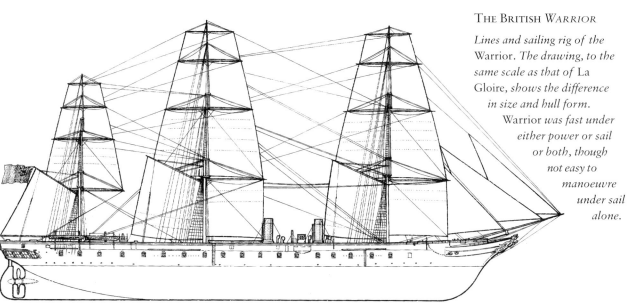

THE BRITISH *WARRIOR*

Lines and sailing rig of the Warrior. *The drawing, to the same scale as that of* La Gloire, *shows the difference in size and hull form.* Warrior *was fast under either power or sail or both, though not easy to manoeuvre under sail alone.*

(oddly, they were designated 'frigates' because Admiralty formulations, based on the number of guns, could not keep up with the pace of technology) on essentially the same plan, which perpetuated the end-to-end gundeck that was characteristic of the first half of the century. But already, under the new Chief Constructor Edward Reed, design was moving on and the centre-battery ship was evolved. This concentrated the main guns, still on the broadside, towards the centre section of the ship where they received maximum protection from increasingly thick iron armour.

Very different things were going on on the other side of the Atlantic. The American Civil War had broken out in 1861 and though it was primarily a land war, its sea aspects were intense, their importance not always fully appreciated by the statesmen and soldiers on either side. The Northern (Union) forces sought to blockade and ultimately control the Southern (Confederate) littoral; the South concentrated on blockade running and commerce raiding. This specialized sea war, the operational aspects of which are covered in Chapter 4, generated new types of ship, of which three were prominent.

The first, the fast blockade-runner, was not a warship and need not concern us much. The other two were both armoured ships. The first, essentially a broadside-firing armoured ship, was typified by the Confederate *Virginia*, previously called the *Merrimac* (this book will employ the more commonly used name – *Virginia*), and later the Northern *New Ironsides*; the second, an entirely new concept in warship design, the Union *Monitor* and her numerous successors.

The *Monitor* was a low-lying, heavily armoured craft, her main feature being an armoured turret designed by a Swedish inventor called Ericsson. She was a tough opponent and a difficult target, and her contest with the *Virginia*, treated in more detail in Chapter 4, was a predictable draw. It was little wonder that the North, with its far superior industrial resources, continued with variations on the 'Monitor' pattern to the extent that by 1865 some forty of such vessels had been built. The South, with a smaller and shrinking industrial base, adapted and armoured existing craft and built a few new ones but to little effect.

But the designs of both American antagonists were much influenced by the circumstances under which they were fighting. The civil war on water was coastal or riverine. That meant seaworthiness was not at a premium, except for the blockade-runners and commerce-raiders. 'Monitors' could have very low freeboard; such ocean passages as they made might be risky, and indeed the original *Monitor* eventually foundered in a seaway. But on rivers all sorts of adaptations or improvisations could be tried. And, in the confined waters of harbours or rivers, there was a great temptation to use an old method of waterborne warfare: ramming.

The ram, in retrospect, is one of the most curious

Warrior preserved at the historic dockyard at Portsmouth, England. Restoration of the ship was carried out at Hartlepool between 1979 and 1987 and the ship has since been presented to the public in a fully authentic state.

Combat between
USS Monitor *and*
CSS Virginia *in Hampton
Roads, 9 March 1862. The
differences in construction
and armament layout are
clearly shown.* Virginia's
*built-up armour gave
her a higher profile with
broadside guns, contrasting
with* Monitor's *low
silhouette and gun turret.*

The only major success for the ram as a weapon of war in the Ironclad Age: the Austrian flagship Ferdinand Max *rams and sinks the Italian battleship* Re d'Italia *at the battle of Lissa, 20 July 1866.*

features of the ironclad period. Yet the reasoning was quite respectable. For the first time since the heyday of the oared galley, a warship was controllable independently of the wind because it now had steam power, and its adversary being heavily clad with iron was vulnerable to being holed under water. Moreover, the alternative means of defeating an opponent – battering with gunfire – might well be ineffective against armour. Therefore – the ram. The theoretical attractions were enhanced in conditions of smooth water and confined areas.

Most of the experience in the American Civil War showed that however good the theory, in practice it did not work very well. Most rammers had insufficient power and manoeuvrability, and most rammees seemed able to alter course, often only just in time, to make the blow a glancing rather than a perpendicular one. When the statistics are considered in cold hindsight, it is clear that the ram was not an effective instrument. Yet ship design persisted with it, not only

in the American Navy but in European navies, for at least three further decades.

The most spectacular success to which advocates of the ram could point was at the battle of Lissa in 1866 when the Austrian flagship *Ferdinand Max* struck the *Re d'Italia*, conveniently stopped broadside on at the time, amidships and sank her. This was the main ammunition for Admiral Sir George Rose Sartorious (a survivor of Trafalgar) in his campaign to make the ram the principal weapon system of the Royal Navy. It was never that; but it was incorporated in every substantial design and indeed the general public often referred to battleships simply as 'rams', as in H. G. Wells's *War of the Worlds* where the most modern of the world's navies steam bravely towards the Martian war machines and are annihilated.

The ram turned out on occasion to be a formidable instrument indeed – unfortunately for sinking one's own side. The *Iron Duke*, a centre-battery

The aftermath of a spectacular ramming incident of 1893, when HMS Camperdown *rammed and sank the British Mediterranean Fleet flagship* Victoria *during a manoeuvre. (This would now be known as 'blue-on-blue'). The Commander-in-Chief, Admiral Sir George Tryon, was lost in the incident, with 357 other personnel.*

ironclad, sank her sister the *Vanguard* in the Irish Sea in 1872 when both ships acted incautiously in a sudden fog. A much more high-profile disaster was the sinking of the *Victoria* by the *Camperdown* in the Mediterranean on 22 June 1893, during a self-evidently dangerous manoeuvre ordered by the Commander-in-Chief Sir George Tryon, who lost his life in the accident.

A feature of the *Vanguard* and *Victoria* sinkings was that both victims were struck in a particularly vulnerable place, at the junction of a transverse bulkhead. That might be thought bad luck; it was probably more germane that damage-control precautions had in both cases been neglected. That might have been a legacy of the good old days of wooden warships, when watertight subdivision was not a feature.

The other development whose first manifestation occurred in the American Civil War was, as already mentioned, the turret-ship. This was a concept which turned out to be much sounder than the ram. The idea of mounting the ship's

HMS CAPTAIN, 1870

A tragically unsuccessful attempt to incorporate gun turrets into a fully-rigged ship, the Captain *capsized in a Bay of Biscay gale after only a few months in operation. Her low freeboard, with poor production control that added weight during building, caused fatal instability.*

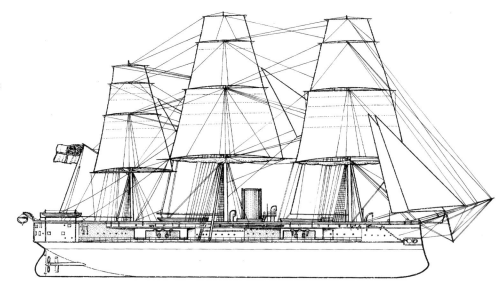

heaviest gun or guns on a turntable that could rotate to fire on any bearing – except, of course, where it would interfere with the structure of one's own ship – had occurred to designers other than Ericsson, notably Captain Cowper Coles of the Royal Navy. Coles's turret design, with the gun mounting rotating on a roller path, was inherently better than Ericsson's which turned on a central stalk, and it was incorporated in a Danish warship, the *Rolf Krake*, in the mid 1860s, and not long after in a radically modified British line-of-battle ship, the *Royal Sovereign*. This ship was for experimental purposes only but much was learnt.

Not, however, enough. An argument broke out between Coles and the Admiralty authorities as to the best design for a full-scale operational turret-ship, and eventually one of each was authorized. Both sides to an extent got it wrong, for both specified a full sailing rig, even though steam technology was becoming more reliable by the year. But with the *Captain* Coles, compounded by the shipbuilders Laird's, got it much more wrong than Reed with the *Monarch*. The

Captain had very low freeboard even as designed, and much lower when completed because of weight added during building; it was calculated that her stability vanished at an angle of heel of not much more than 40 degrees. Yet she was the darling of the Press, whom Coles had assiduously wooed. On the first two or three occasions she went to sea she seemed to behave well enough, but she capsized in a Bay of Biscay gale on 6 September 1870.

The *Monarch* by contrast was stable and seaworthy, though she did not handle well under sail alone. Reed, her designer, never much liked the concept, and was much happier with his first 'mastless' turret-ship, the *Devastation*, which came into service only a short time after the *Monarch* in 1871. This vessel was the prototype of the Victorian battleship as the world came to know it: of low profile, broad-beamed, heavily armoured, its main guns in twin turrets forward and aft, with only a 'military mast' for flag-signalling and no motive power other than steam.

In spite of the pattern that was then set, hull design proceeded by fits and starts for the next two decades, which have rightly been called the 'groping age' in warship design. Partly this was due to a belt-and-braces attitude in the users: they did not want to move to a navy reliant entirely on steam, a development which was

This idealized picture of the Captain *off Gibraltar illustrates the high regard in which the public held the ship and her designer, Captain Cowper Coles, who lost his life when she went down a few months later.*

considered too risky for them to contemplate. In consequence some battleships continued to appear during the 1870s with full sailing rigs which looked increasingly incongruous; at least one ship, *Inflexible*, the pride of the fleet, had instructions to ditch all masts and sails if she went into action. Turrets, too, were not regarded as the only sensible way of deploying big guns; the broadside battery was still favoured by many, and centre-battery ships were brought into service for several years after the appearance of the *Devastation*. The belt-and-braces approach was carried furthest in the *Temeraire*, a fully brig-rigged ship with centre-battery guns and two turrets. This ultimate hybrid came into service in 1877.

Things were no less tentatively managed on the Continent. The French built only eight battleships in the 1870s, less than half the number achieved by the British and of equally experimental design. The Russians were exceptionally enterprising, building some craft of extraordinary design culminating in the charmingly named 'popoffkas', almost completely round in plan. The Italians under their great designer Benedetto Brin produced some fast, powerful battleships that certainly influenced thinking worldwide, including Britain. Brin's attitude to armour was of particular interest: he favoured a central citadel with very little armour at either bow or stern, and this pattern was in essence adopted by the British chief designer Barnaby for some years around 1880 – much

HMS Devastation, *the first mastless battleship, designed by Sir Edward Reed. While her breastwork layout and low freeboard might have made her unsuitable for ocean fighting, she was well adapted to defence and attack of naval bases, which figured prominently in 1870s strategy.*

to the chagrin of Reed, who had retired but voiced dissent from the sidelines.

Other navies did not at that period amount to much. The Americans had ceased building large ships altogether; the Germans had scarcely begun to think of a fleet; the Chinese and Japanese had no more than token forces. In these circumstances, with the British battle fleet dominant, the smaller ships of the Royal Navy could expect much freedom of action and their design reflected that

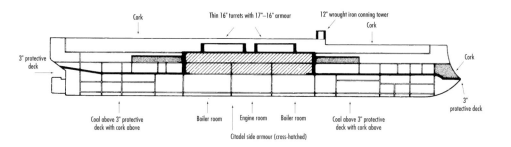

Cork

Thin 16" turrets with 17"–16" armour

12" wrought iron conning tower

Cork

3" protective deck

Cork

3" protective deck

Coal above 3" protective deck with cork above

Boiler room

Engine room

Boiler room

Coal above 3" protective deck with cork above

Citadel side armour (cross-hatched)

The armour scheme of HMS Inflexible, 1881

This Barnaby-designed ship adopted the principle of a heavily armoured central citadel with relatively weakly protected ends. The laminated wrought-iron and teak side armour amounted to one of the heaviest and thickest protective layers ever

mounted – though not the strongest, since steel was soon to supersede iron armour. This ship used steam extensively to power auxiliary and domestic machinery, and electricity was used generally for lighting for the first time.

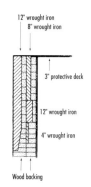

12" wrought iron

8" wrought iron

3" protective deck

12" wrought iron

4" wrought iron

Wood backing

Centrepiece of this display of British naval power in 1897 was the 'Royal Sovereign' class of battleships, designed by Sir William White. They were soundly based and could fulfil all battle-fleet roles in both ocean and coastal waters.

Continental navies quickly followed Britain and France into ironclad technology. The Spanish broadside ironclad frigate Numancia, *built in France, was in service by 1863. She figured prominently in the turbulent early years of the South American republics and was the first ironclad to circumnavigate the world.*

confidence. Seaworthy, conventional, with adequate firepower, the cruisers and gunboats were able to go about their work without too much regard for sophisticated opposition.

By the late 1880s everything was beginning to change. The mastless battleship now held sway. The British 'Admiral' class, though limited in a seaway because of their low freeboard, were at least the equal of anything else afloat, but other countries, notably France and Russia, were stirring, and France was using steel for construction well in advance of Britain. The British, spurred on by the 'navalist' movement led by W. T. Stead, reacted with a speed that would not have been possible without their highly developed shipbuilding and engineering industries.

The stage was set for the advent of Sir William White as Chief Constructor.

He had been Barnaby's deputy and had learned in a hard school. In the programmes set out in the Naval Act of 1889 White's designs, solid, reliable, progressive and homogeneous, soon showed in classes not only of battleships but of cruisers. (Destroyers were left to private contractors to bid for; they were still experimental.) Armour now was face-hardened by the Harvey or Krupp processes; its resistance was greater by far than iron or previous compounds, and less weight was therefore needed. The consequence was perhaps the most stately steam-powered fleet ever seen: the 'Royal Sovereign', 'Majestic' and 'Canopus' classes quartered the Mediterranean, the Atlantic and the China Station, not simply a symbol but an instrument of British power. Behind that deterrent shield the cruisers – ranging from monsters like the *Powerful* and *Terrible* to 3,000-ton ships of the 'Apollo' class – could do the work of defending, or acquiring, Empire.

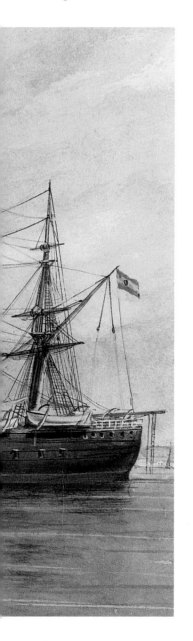

In hindsight, the challenges may not have been particularly severe in the decade up to 1900. Certainly the French were building battleships again, after their flirtation with a truly radical concept of naval operations under the *Jeune École*, and the Americans, spurred on by the theories of Mahan and the politics of Theodore Roosevelt, had embarked on a massive programme. The Russians, Japanese and Chinese were arming, though not it appeared against Britain so much as against each other; and much of their construction was taking place in British or Western European yards. But there was no doubt that the pace of construction had much increased, swept on as much by the new-found confidence in *matériel* and design as by any political will or theory of sea power.

The final phase of the Ironclad Age in ship construction was indeed brief. The five years from 1900 were marked, as is well known, by the rise of the Imperial German Navy, Tirpitz's 'Risk Fleet'. German industry had made great strides since the unification of the country under Bismarck, and once the decision was made by the Kaiser to develop a powerful navy, progress was extremely rapid. The British response was swift and effective, and British hull design culminated in the *Dreadnought*, a ship that properly brought the Ironclad Age to its end.

OVERLEAF: *All major navies began to build rapidly in the 1890s, making the balance of sea power theoretically far less stable than it had been. French, American, German and Russian battleships all demonstrated the different strategic and tactical concepts of their owners but all strove to achieve balance between armament, armour, speed and stability.*

French battleship *Henri IV*

Russian battleship *Georgi Pobiedonosetz*

US battleship *Connecticut*

German battleship *Schwaben*

LIFTING PROPELLER

HMS Warrior's *lifting propeller. To improve ship handling when under sail alone, the propeller could be disconnected from its drive shaft and hauled up into the hull by means of a chain.*

HMS Warrior's *engine. This Penn single-cylinder trunk engine was a conventional design for its time but reliably propelled the ship when under steam at a hitherto unprecedented speed for a major warship of 14 knots.*

PROPULSION

HMS *Warrior*'s maximum speed under steam was 14 $\frac{1}{2}$ knots. This was a step change: previously, admirals had been accustomed to think of fleet speeds of advance of perhaps 5 or 6 knots, and if the wind was foul even that would be a struggle and could be sustained only for the period that fuel stocks allowed. Now the possibility opened up of naval forces – even those having to keep ample speed margins for station-keeping, possible breakdowns and sub-standard fuel quality – moving towards their objectives at up to 10 knots. It would not happen overnight, but it was a reasonable prospect.

But as the broadside ironclads – *Black Prince*, *Defence*, *Resistance*, *Hector* and the rest – slid down the ways in the early to mid 1860s, they were still considered by many as sailing ships with auxiliary power. All carried full sailing rigs; indeed the *Agincourt* at one time had five masts, the most ever mounted in a warship. Most had hoistable propellers, to enhance manoeuvrability under sail alone; 'up funnel' might no longer be a feasible order, but 'down screw' was. Little by little, however, captains and admirals in the battle fleet were coming to rely on their machinery to keep them moving in the desired direction.

The trend continued in the centre-battery ships, *Bellerophon* (1865) and her successors. The midships grouping of the main armament enabled Reed, her designer, to produce a shorter, handier ship than the 'Warrior' type which carried guns the whole length of the gundeck in the way that had been traditional for nearly three hundred years; the penalty in the centre-battery ships was increased power:weight ratio and somewhat slower speed under sail alone.

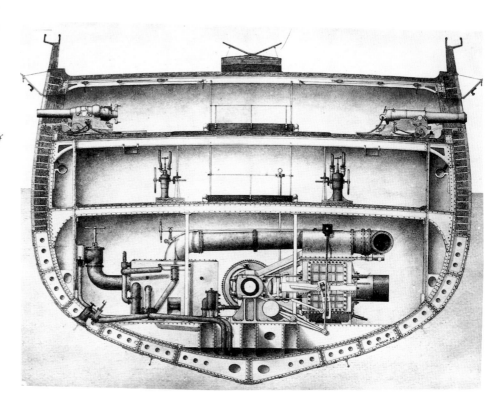

Even the advent of turret-ships, the *Monarch* and the ill-fated *Captain*, did not immediately wean the Admiralty away from a perceived necessity for sail. Both carried full sailing rigs and it was of course sail that aided the *Captain*'s capsize, even though her instability and lack of freeboard were the primary causes.

But the writing was on the wall, as much for operational as for safety reasons. The masts of the *Monarch*, necessarily bulky and heavily stayed, were impediments to all-round fire and particularly to end-on fire, thought to be an important component of ramming tactics. In the *Captain* it had been sought to overcome this difficulty by fitting tripod masts, but these carried their own disadvantages.

The solution was to bite the bullet and admit that turrets and full sailing rig were incompatible. It was much to the credit of Barnaby the designer, and Spencer Robinson the Controller of the Navy, that the first 'mastless' battleship, the *Devastation*, was in service as early as 1871. Henceforth sail in battleships, if fitted at all, was an auxiliary to steam power and not the other way about.

One of the developments that made this possible was the increasing efficiency of boilers and engines. The *Warrior* was fitted with a Penn two-cylinder single-expansion trunk engine, to which steam was supplied normally at 15 pounds per square inch by up to ten smoke-tube boilers. At 11 knots she consumed $3\frac{1}{2}$ tons of coal per hour, this rising to nearly three times that amount at her maximum speed. Her range under steam alone, given her bunker capacity of some 850 tons, was barely enough to get her across the Atlantic even at economical speed.

SWEABORG,
8–10 AUGUST 1855

Though no ironclads were present, the other two features of the Ironclad Age – steam and shellfire – were essential elements in this fierce and effective bombardment of the Russian fortress of Sweaborg in the Baltic. A carefully planned and highly organized allied operation, based upon extensive surveys and reconnaissance, made maximum use of the extended range of mortars carried in specially constructed vessels, and the diversionary capabilities of steam-powered gunboats.

HMS Monarch, *1871. A high-freeboard turret-ship, much safer than the ill-fated* Captain, *she nevertheless suffered from the belt-and-braces approach that gave her a full sailing rig as well as steam power. Note the massive construction of the masts, an impediment to fighting ability.*

Helsingfors

Second day:
Allied gunboats

Allied gunboats

Allied gunboats

Oterhall

British mortar vessels

Skogsholm

Dragon

Euryalus

French mortar vessels

Skogskar

Vulture

Magicienne

Allied fleet at anchor

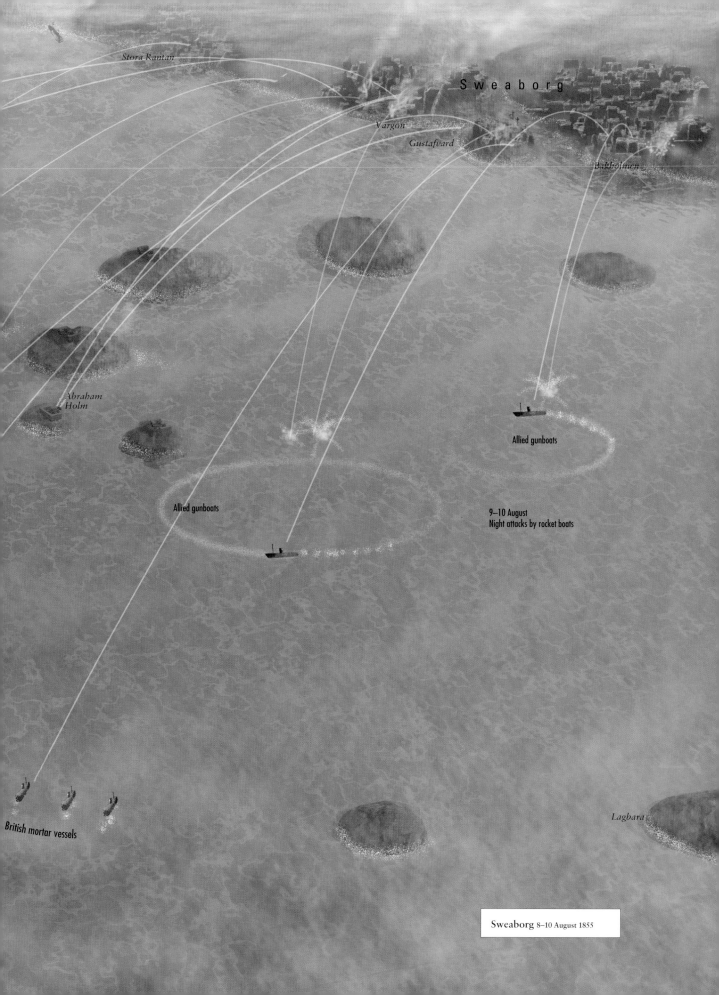

Stora Rantan

Sweaborg

Vargon

Gustafvard

Balholmen

Abraham
Holm

Allied gunboats

Allied gunboats

9–10 August
Night attacks by rocket boats

British mortar vessels

Lagbara

Sweaborg 8–10 August 1855

More advanced engines, making better use of steam supplied from the boilers, were not fitted to battleships until they had been in service for some years in the merchant navy and smaller warships. The compound engine, right, was introduced according to this principle.

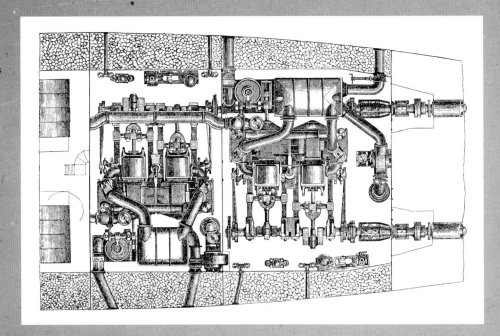

Over the next three decades efficiencies steadily improved in all aspects of steam propulsion. There were two factors that helped this rapid advance. First, the engineering industry was intensely competitive. Firms such as Maudslay, Penn, Napier, Humphrys and Ravenhill competed eagerly for Admiralty contracts, and all aspects of performance were under constant scrutiny. Second, the Admiralty, although unlikely to invent devices on its own account – indeed, it had no establishment capable of doing so – kept a careful eye on innovations, particularly in the merchant fleet, and conducted trials in naval ships where these were thought to point the way of progress.

Thus, in the field of steam engines, the obvious successor to the single-expansion trunk engine – the two-stage engine with high- and low-pressure cylinders – began to be fitted in the merchant fleet from 1855 onwards, but it was not till about 1870, after trials that had lasted half a decade, that it was decided to fit these compound engines in battleships. Similarly, the next stage of development, the triple-expansion engine whose principle lasted as long as reciprocating steam engines did, was introduced in the merchant navy around

The final major development of steam-powered engines was the turbine, designed by Charles Parsons in the 1880s and fitted in the experimental vessel Turbinia, below, in the mid 1890s. She caused a sensation at the 1897 Diamond Jubilee Review and steam turbines were soon the prime movers even of major warships.

1880, tried out in the torpedo gunboat *Rattlesnake* in 1885 and first fitted to battleships *Victoria* and *Sans Pareil* in 1889.

A graphic example of the advantages of triple expansion is given by the figures for the *Thunderer*, a sister of the *Devastation*, built in 1872 and modernized in 1889–90. On a measured run to Madeira, which seems to have been a favoured racetrack for such trials, the modernized ship consumed a little less than half the fuel she would previously have used. Moreover, it was claimed that her original engines, even when new, would never have stood the strain of such a sustained run.

A final steam-engine innovation, though it comes only just within the time frame of this book, must be mentioned here. The steam turbine, invented by Charles Parsons in the mid 1880s, was a working proposition by 1895, and in 1897 his experimental vessel, *Turbinia*, raced up and down the lines of the fleets assembled for Queen Victoria's Diamond Jubilee Review at Spithead. It has been suggested that Sir John Durston, the Engineer in Chief of the Royal Navy, far from being scandalized, had done much to encourage Parsons and was privy to the demonstration. Turbine propulsion was quickly fitted thereafter to several classes of destroyer and its adoption for the battleship *Dreadnought* (1905) sealed the package for all fast steam-driven ships for many generations.

None of these advances could have been made without the development of boilers producing ever higher steam pressures and steadily improving steam quality. There are three basic ways of producing steam. The first, applying an external heat source to an enclosed body of water – a simple kettle – was too dangerous and inefficient to use at sea. The second method was to lead hot tubes through a body of water, so making it boil and produce steam; this was a smoke-tube or fire-tube boiler. The third was the reverse process, leading tubes of water through a heat source so that the water in the tubes was brought to boiling point; this was a water-tube boiler.

Fire-tube boilers, as in the 'Scotch boiler' shown in the diagram, were the standard means of producing steam up to the 1880s. Heated pipes ran through the water jacket turning the briny water into steam.

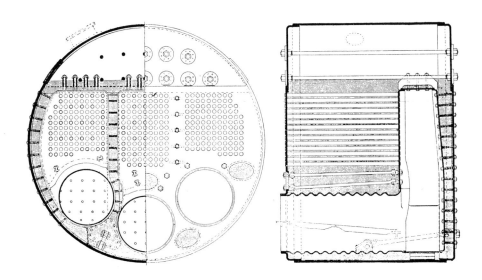

In the Royal Navy fire-tube boilers were fitted for the whole of the three decades from 1860 to 1890. This did not mean boiler technology had stood still during that time. In the *Warrior* the basic feed for the boilers was sea water, but the water in the boiler was in fact brackish; as it produced steam it became more and more briny and every few hours some of it would have to be blown down, with consequent reduction of boiler pressure, and replaced with condensate – pure water condensed from exhaust steam from the engine.

The first refinement then had to be a reduction in the brine component in the feed, reducing the need to blow down and giving a chance of working the boilers at higher pressure. This was achieved by sophistication of design, by the increasing use of steel in boiler construction and by the general introduction of the surface condenser which greatly assisted the purity of boiler feed.

A boost to boiler power was provided by forced draught. This was a system whereby the stokehold was closed and air supplied by fans increased the atmospheric pressure, thus feeding the grate area and making the coal burn more quickly, with a consequent increase in steam pressure. Between 1880 and 1895 forced draught was a generally fitted feature. It was not intended for routine use but for action or emergency conditions. In general the use of forced draught gave the ship an extra knot or so of maximum speed, at the expense of higher fuel consumption and more or less frenzied labour – in worse environmental conditions than for natural draught – for the stokers. There was some suspicion about forced draught throughout the naval community. Many thought it was straining after a gnat.

Relief was at hand in the water-tube boiler. This was one area where the continental navies were years ahead of the British. In France, Belleville had developed a working boiler of this type by 1880, and during the decade it was fitted in all vessels of the *Messageries Maritimes*, the French mail shipping line, and adopted for the French Navy in 1889. The British, by now impressed, ordered Bellevilles for the massive fast cruisers *Powerful* and *Terrible* (themselves 'answers' to the Russian *Rurik* and *Rossiya*) in 1892.

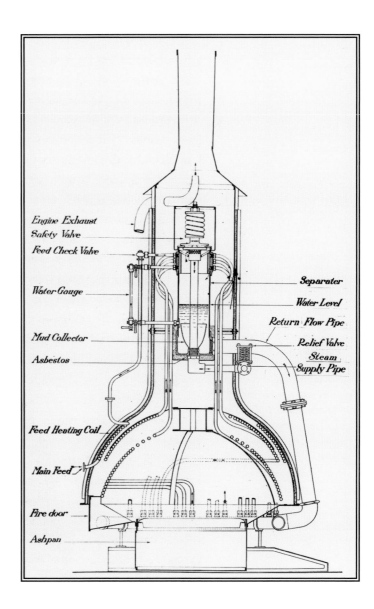

An early design of water-tube boiler, which, by leading water through pipes exposed to heat, reversed the fire-tube principle. French design generally marched ahead of British through the 1880s in this area.

These boilers delivered steam at 260 pounds per square inch, a very marked advance on all previous installations. It was not achieved without a reliability cost. Neither technology nor, in Britain, training were ready for such a high-pressure system, and leaks leading to dramatic reductions in designed efficiency were widespread. Moreover, proponents of the fire-tube boiler – which in its final form of the 'Scotch Boiler' had reached a plateau of efficiency – were well entrenched and backed, of course, by its manufacturers. Controversy continued throughout the 1890s and culminated in the so-called Battle of the Boilers which lasted from 1901 to 1904. By then several British designs of water-tube boiler were in service, and after exhaustive enquiry – aided no doubt by understandable if unjustified chauvinism – the Admiralty settled on the Babcock and Wilcox and Yarrow as suitable water-tube boilers for the Royal Navy, and the Yarrow was developed into the Admiralty Three Drum Boiler so well known to engineers between the two World Wars.

But for all the increases in efficiency of steam production and machinery during the Ironclad Age there was one enduring, pervasive factor: coal. There was

For the more remote stations, with coal supplies scattered and unreliable, sail was still an essential element of mobility. Even in the 1890s cruisers such as HMS Calypso still required full sailing rig.

no other fuel available throughout the period; oil was not introduced, even experimentally, until near its very end. The effects of coal on strategic planning, on operations and on naval ethos will be traced in subsequent chapters. Here it is necessary simply to say that the arrangements for stowage of the fuel were an important component of ship design, and the amount carried was of course a crucial factor in the range a ship could traverse without replenishing.

In some designs coal was regarded as an adjunct to armour. Two feet of coal was regarded as equivalent to an inch of steel, and bunkers were often situated as much for this purpose as for convenience of access. Even less prominent in design was convenience of replenishment. Merchant ships' bunkers were designed for coaling from fixed installations in shore berths, but warships had plenty of on-board labour and operational ships would not usually go alongside for coaling; it was far more likely that they would be supplied by lighters or colliers out in the stream and coal manhandled on board.

The availability of coal worldwide had important effects on ship design. Battleships generally were expected to operate in the more developed parts of the

By 1900, with more widespread coal stocks, even cruisers lost their sailing rigs except for auxiliary purposes. The Russian 'Rurik' class were regarded as fast, menacing threats which required counters from other powers.

world where coal stocks either existed or could readily be brought to them by hired colliers. Cruisers and gunboats were in a different situation. They would often be operating in remote parts, carrying out unforeseen tasks. In consequence, they were fitted with masts and sails long after these had been relinquished for battleships, and records exist of cruisers in the 1890s that spent the great majority of their passage-time under sail alone.

That was, however, the last gasp of the sailing navy. By 1900 cruisers had acquired a shape that remained familiar up to the end of the Second World War: steamships of a certain stateliness even if they did not have the overt power of battleships, relatively fast, of great range but limited firepower. In the last decade of the century, many nations could claim the lead in cruiser construction at various times and in various aspects: the French with the 'Kléber' class, the Russians with the theoretically fast and powerful 'Rurik', the Americans with the 'Brooklyn' and the Japanese with the 'Asama' classes. However, British industry and design capacity were well able, at this stage, to outbuild any competitor, and if one or other could claim superiority in operation of its machinery (as has frequently been claimed by historians of the French Navy) this was countered by British preponderance in numbers. Britain's economy was still half as great again as that of France, and well ahead of that of Germany. It would not last, but that was how it was at the time.

Armament

The *Warrior*, when first commissioned, was armed on the main deck with thirty 68-pounder muzzle-loading smoothbore cannon and eight 110-pounder Armstrong breech-loaders. In addition she had upper-deck armament ranging from 110-pounder breech-loaders to 6-pounder cannon.

This heavy and varied armament could deploy a very wide range of ammunition types. The 68-pounders had the option of three sorts of shot – the traditional cannonball, case or canister which on shattering delivered ninety iron balls for anti-personnel purposes, and grape which similarly delivered some fifteen larger balls – and three of shell, one with a simple gunpowder explosion, the second of shrapnel with 340 balls delivered on explosion of a time-fuse, and the third a device called the Martin's shell holding molten iron borne to the gun from a furnace on board (said to be safer than red-hot shot). The 110-pounders were almost as versatile, with two shot and two shell options.

Effective range and rate of fire had, however, changed little since the days of Nelson. A crack ship of the line of 1805, her crews battle-hardened, could fire three broadsides in five minutes. The *Warrior*, with large guns' crews trained in the school in the *Excellent* founded in 1830, could manage one a minute, with the Armstrongs firing a fraction faster. As for effective range, the smoothbores were

Gundeck layout

The gundeck layout of HMS Warrior. *While some new models of gun were fitted, including a few breech-loaders, and sighting methods were improved, the ship was still essentially designed for broadside fire like that of a line-of-battle ship.*

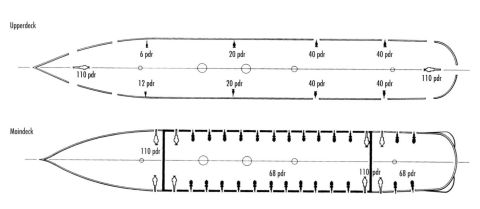

little use outside a mile, while the Armstrongs could fire out to a maximum of just over twice that.

All in all, then, the *Warrior*'s was a formidable and innovative battery, and combined with her armour and mobility it made her more than a match for anything else afloat. Pride, however, and there was plenty, was always tempered with caution, and it was caution that soon got the upper hand at the British Admiralty so far as arming the fleet was concerned.

The main problem concerned the breech-loading guns. These were extensively tested during the *Warrior*'s first commission and the general report was favourable, particularly on range and accuracy. But warnings were sounded about the danger of premature explosion and accidents with the firing mechanism, and the Select Committee on Ordnance took note of them. Their fears were confirmed when, at the bombardment of Kagoshima in 1863, twenty-eight accidents were reported in a total of 365 rounds fired by twenty-one breech-loading guns. These were, of course, from a number of different ships, none of them so well worked-up, nor with such picked crews, as the *Warrior*.

In consequence, the breech-loader, in its then form of a fully screwed breech with vent tube firing, was suspect. The Royal Navy reacted not by endeavouring rapidly to improve the breech-loader, but by restoring the muzzle-loader to its former dominance.

To be sure, it was a much improved muzzle-loader. Rifling – spiral grooves inside the gun barrel – had long been known to be desirable because by imparting a spin to the projectile it improved accuracy. Now it became standard, studs in the shot or shell engaging in the grooves. The guns were increasingly carried on iron (later steel) carriages, rather than wood, to improve shock resistance and durability. Hydraulic machinery was introduced to absorb recoil and run-out, and to assist in loading. As calibres increased and projectiles became heavier, it was absolutely necessary to aid the

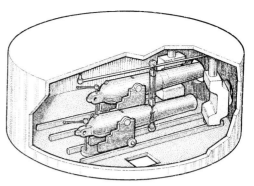

GUN TURRET

The gun turret of USS Monitor, 1862. The muzzle-loading 11-inch guns could be loaded from inside the turret after recoil. Blanking plates moved across the embrasures to protect the crew during loading. Rate of fire was very slow, about one round every 15 minutes.

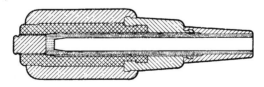

MUZZLE-LOADING RIFLED GUN

Cross section of the British 12-inch, 35-ton muzzle-loading rifled gun (RML), the standard weapon of British battleships in the 1870s and early 1880s.

TURRET MACHINERY

Turret machinery and construction became steadily more sophisticated throughout the Ironclad Age. Muzzle-loaders in particular needed elaborate arrangements. The diagram shows the gearing and roller-path design that enabled the Monarch's turret to traverse.

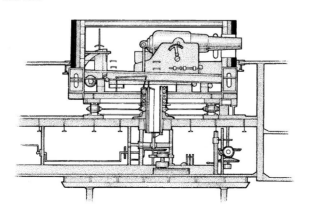

loaders (who of course had to stand in front of the smoking barrels in order to load) in this way.

The rifled muzzle-loader (RML) could be accommodated in a barbette – a kind of armoured revetment with an open top, the guns turning inside it – or a turret, the now more familiar battleship mounting, roofed and trainable as a whole. In each case the guns would have short barrels, since however elaborate the loading arrangements the mouth of the barrel had to be accessible. For loading it was nearly always necessary to bring the guns to full depression and often to train them fore and aft as well.

So the RML had inherent limitations. Its rate of fire was slow, slower even than that of Nelson's ships of the line; *Inflexible*, the premier ship of the fleet that bombarded Alexandria in 1882, managed one round per gun every three minutes. The RML's short barrel made it unsuitable for the slow-burning but immensely more powerful propellants that were coming into service in the late 1870s. And, on top of this, it was beginning to look more dangerous in operation

PIVOT MECHANISM

Breech-loading gun on disappearing pivot mount, 1870s. This complicated design aimed to make loading easier and to protect guns' crews, but was not widely adopted.

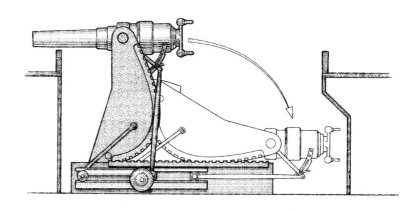

Early breech-loading guns employed a fully screwed breech which could cause operating and safety problems for undertrained crews. Accidents during the bombardment of Kagoshima, 1863, led to a loss of confidence in breech-loaders.

than the breech-loaders that had been generally fitted in continental navies for several years.

The catalyst was a fatal explosion in one of the guns of the *Thunderer* in 1879. This was caused by double-loading: two propellant cartridges had been put into the gun. That was an error which physically could not have occurred in a breech-loader, and it spurred the Royal Navy into change. But this was a long time coming; it was not until the mid 1880s that a reliable breech-loader was developed, and even then guns were of diverse manufacture and design. Moreover, in early models the breech still had to be unscrewed and completely removed between one firing of the gun and the next; the device of a breech that swung on hinges and, on closing, engaged its half-screw with a half-screw in the barrel of the gun was not in full service until the 1890s. In consequence, the rate of fire of these early breech-loaders was still slow – about one round every two minutes.

Nevertheless, it was high time the British adopted the system. The French,

The standard breech-loading mechanism from about 1890, employing a hinged breech with a half-screw which turns to engage in a similar half-screw in the barrel itself.

with their 13.4-inch 'Model 1870', had been years ahead of the British, and the shortcomings of French *matériel* had been much less apparent in the weapons than in the ships that carried them. The Italians had encouraged British gun designers to produce for them weapons that were unacceptable to the much more conservative British Ordnance Board. While some experiments conducted by the Royal Navy had suggested that muzzle-loaders were not inferior in penetration of standard armour than breech-loaders of similar calibre, the portents had clearly been in favour of the breech-loader for years.

As was usual in this period, once the British had decided to catch up they did so with some speed. Even so, it was not until the early 1890s that they could be said to match the continental powers, and Clowes – a near-contemporary historian – said, 'it should ever be a subject of congratulation that, during the many years when the transition was in the process of accomplishment, the British Navy never had to measure itself with one of the great navies which, ere Britain had begun to move in the matter, had completed their rearmament'.

Meanwhile, other aberrations had persisted. There was, as it would seem to us today, an absurd obsession with end-on fire. This was partly due to a simplistic emphasis on the offensive, but was rationalized by residual reliance on the ram as a weapon. If you were going for your enemy in the belly, you needed to shoot at him on the way in. In the later centre-battery ships this had entailed recessed ports for some of the guns, which could thereby, in theory, fire right ahead. In fact, as in the *Alexandra* (1879), grandest of the centre-battery ships, these guns were so wet in any sort of head sea that they could be fired only with the greatest difficulty. In turret- and barbette ships, shorn of any sailing rig, right-ahead fire was designed in, either by mounting turrets in echelon or by designing a very low forecastle, usually both. This meant washing down in a head sea, which in turn made loading and firing difficult. On the continent, particularly in the Mediterranean navies, there was even more emphasis on arcs of fire and 'four-cornered' ships with single turrets were designed to give maximum theoretical impact, without much guarantee that they would have made sense in action. The attractions of the ram had much to answer for.

Ammunition, and its handling and stowage, was always a worry and became more so as propellants and shell fillings were increasingly powerful and volatile. At the bombardment of Alexandria the Gunner of the *Alexandra* earned a Victoria Cross for dowsing in a bucket of water a shell, fired by one of the forts, that had just landed in the long ammunition path between the magazine and the guns. In doing so he probably saved the ship. In later designs, particularly the barbette and turret-ships, the layout was more logical, with magazines situated beneath the mountings and under armour, but the problems were never entirely solved as the losses at Jutland years later, and several harbour accidents before and after that battle, showed. They were not confined to the Royal Navy; the French *Iena* was similarly lost in the 1890s and many historians contend that USS *Maine*, whose explosion in Havana sparked the Spanish–American War in 1898, blew up from the same cause rather than from Spanish sabotage.

The gun-armament situation was complicated from about 1880 onwards by the increasing tendency, in all navies, to fit a comprehensive secondary armament. This ranged from 9.2-inch guns supplementing the 12-inch in some battleships, to Nordenfelt and Maxim 0.45-inch machine-guns, and included a gamut of calibres and designs most of which could be designated as quick-firers.

There were several reasons for this proliferation of above-water weaponry, which was not confined to battleships but extended pro rata to cruisers. There was general dissatisfaction with the slow rate of fire of the main guns. Even a 9.2 could keep up a higher rate than a 12-inch, and guns from the 6-inch on down could fire rapidly enough to keep an enemy distracted at the kind of ranges that were in prospect. This led to the 'hail-of-fire' concept which suggested that at fighting ranges, fire from all arms could actually be intense enough to drive enemy guns' crews away from their mountings; in later chapters we shall see how this theory fared. Finally, however, there was a self-defensive role for secondary armament, and this had arisen because of the advent of a new menace to ships that had previously worked on the principle that like fought like: the torpedo.

The locomotive torpedo was designed by Robert Whitehead, an Englishman who had worked in various European countries from the age of 16 and by the time he was 40 had set up a factory in Fiume, with close links with the Austrian government and navy. He developed a system of depth-keeping for a submerged torpedo which was known as 'the Secret' and was eagerly sought by all the major navies. Whitehead, a shrewd businessman, refused to sell the Secret to one nation alone; when he sold it, it was understood that it was a non-exclusive right. Thus in 1872 both Britain and France acquired it within a year of each other, and several other nations followed suit. Twenty years later there was still considerable security surrounding the principle, but it was by now so widely known that it could be called a Secret no longer. By then, however, Whitehead had done very nicely. The soundness of his scientific thinking is demonstrated by the fact that torpedoes up to and after the Second World War still kept depth essentially by the device invented by Whitehead: a hydrostat-pendulum combination that applied damped signals to the elevators controlling the torpedo's angle up and down, thus keeping the torpedo to its set depth within very narrow limits.

Early Whitehead torpedoes were of very limited range, the Fiume 14-inch Mark I managing only 600 yards at $17^1/_2$ knots. Yet their potential was quickly recognized in all major naval countries although the reasoning was not the same in every case.

The French, probably the most enthusiastic of all, saw a possibility of reversing the preponderance of Britain by the leverage that could be brought by rapid development of the torpedo. They saw a twin requirement: to protect their bases and to attack enemy commerce, and both these missions, it was believed, would be helped by torpedo craft. All kinds of ideas were tried: battleships fitted with torpedoes as supplements to the ram, mother-ships to transport torpedo boats to remote areas, and of course numerous torpedo craft to deploy their weapons in the harbour defence role.

The other continental powers, the Americans and the Japanese all began with ideas similar to those of the French, but tended away from commerce raiding

HMS Hornet, *a torpedo boat destroyer of 1894. Originally conceived as a counter to raiding torpedo boats, destroyers soon carried torpedoes themselves. They were the subject of intense competition between rival shipbuilders who strove for speed and armament, often at the expense of structural integrity.*

and towards the use of torpedoes in fleet action as well as harbour defence.

British enthusiasm, never too easy to whip up in favour of a new weapon, was pushed on by a number of personalities. The initiator was Vice Admiral Lord Clarence Paget, whose report in 1868 first alerted the Admiralty to what was going on in Fiume. Soon afterwards 'Jacky' Fisher, then a commander, showed interest in the potential of the torpedo and wrote a number of papers on the subject. He was appointed to the *Excellent* as Torpedo Instructor in 1872 and in 1876 a separate Torpedo School was established in the *Vernon*, thanks to the encouragement of a number of senior officers as well as the advocacy of Fisher himself. In the meantime, the Royal Navy had bought a large number of torpedoes from Fiume as well as manufacturing them at home, and they were being fitted widely in existing craft as well as in some that were specially designed.

Of these the most bizarre was the 'torpedo ram' *Polyphemus*, a cigar-shaped, semi-submerged vessel of over 2,500 tons, which carried five torpedoes that went no faster than her own maximum speed of $17\frac{1}{2}$ knots. But of course it was not intended that her approach to a target would be anything but slow and furtive; she was indeed a 'stealth' vessel, until surprise had been achieved by torpedo attack and her speed could be used to follow up with the ram. While hailed by some as a future war-winner, and scoring one spectacular success in an 1885 exercise, the *Polyphemus* was not followed by any similar design.

The mainstream of torpedo craft design lay in the fast torpedo boat. The first of these to be built in Britain, the *Lightning*, was a prime example of

collaboration between the Admiralty and private industry, built and engined by Thornycroft in 1876. She was followed by a generation of boats which, while suitable for sheltered waters, were inadequate in a seaway. Size then inevitably increased, but so did the scale of the countermeasures. These were in two main forms: the diversity of secondary armaments in major units, already mentioned, and the evolution of gun-armed smaller vessels to catch and destroy torpedo boats – the destroyers, which were themselves soon armed with torpedoes as well.

It was in this class of ship, built from about 1892 onwards, that can most clearly be seen the effect of intense competition between a large number of firms as moderated and modified by the Constructor's Department in the Admiralty. Designs were diverse among the builders involved and so were armaments, propulsion units and accommodation, but some commonality was achieved through the efforts of the Assistant Director of Naval Construction, Henry Deadman. There was constant striving after speed, often to the detriment of structural strength, machinery reliability and seakeeping. How effective these destroyers would have been in a fleet action under ocean conditions is uncertain.

The French Navy initially developed torpedo craft even more rapidly than the British; by 1883, it is said, France had fifty to Britain's nineteen. That was the natural outcome of French enthusiasm for this potential 'equalizer' of the naval balance. But it was comparatively short-lived. From the late 1880s French naval construction policy was bedevilled by bitter controversy between the *Jeune École* and the traditionalists, and moreover there was an economic recession in France that lasted most of the succeeding decade. Russia, Japan, Italy and

A spar torpedo mounted in a steam launch. Both sides in the American Civil War had some success with such torpedoes but the advent of the self-propelled Whitehead cut down plans for their general use.

Germany also embraced the torpedo boat and later the destroyer concept with enthusiasm, and many were built, with varying degrees of success and seaworthiness.

The locomotive torpedo, then, as an underwater weapon helped to turn sea warfare from a two-dimensional to a three-dimensional art. But there were other devices that sought to work in the same direction.

Two other forms of propelled torpedo proved of little operational value and were in due course discarded. One was the spar torpedo, carried on the bows of

CONFEDERATE MINE

A Confederate mine of the American Civil War. The Hertz Horn method of detonating mines on contact had not yet been invented and electrical detonation from shore, or unreliable impact fuses, were common.

a suicidally inclined small boat. It had had some limited success in the hands of both sides in the American Civil War, and was tried in exercises throughout the 1870s as a weapon of surprise, but the autonomous Whitehead had such clear advantages in this role that it soon gained credence. Even less effective was the towed torpedo, which was designed to be pulled equally suicidally across the path of an advancing vessel. Experiments continued throughout the 1870s but the towed torpedo never entered general service, to the relief of all concerned.

A far more serious underwater weapon was the immobile mine. The idea of

Attack on and defence of harbours were major preoccupations of naval powers in the 1870s and 1880s. Torpedo boats of all kinds, mines and boom defences all featured, as in this view of a demonstration in 1879.

a device which would explode under a ship was much older than ironclads, and the earliest systematic treatment was in the Napoleonic Wars when Robert Fulton had conducted operational tests both in Britain and America. In the Russian War of 1854–6 there was extensive use of ground mines by the Russians; these were generally called 'infernal machines' by their opponents, with more than a whiff of accusation that they were unsportsmanlike. By the outbreak of the American Civil War, therefore, mine technology was widespread, and in that war proved capable of all kinds of adaptation and improvisation. Mines whose explosion was controlled by electric cables from the shore, and mines which blew up on contact, were supplemented by all kinds of devices laid particularly by the Confederates, whose coastline and harbours were most at risk. In all thirty-two Union ships were sunk by mines during the war – far more than were accounted for by ramming or gunfire.

With this data, which was freely available during and after the Civil War, it is surprising that Western European navies did not make more provision for mine warfare in the next few decades. Even when the Hertz Horn mine, with its reliable method of detonation on contact, made its appearance in the mid 1870s the British shied away from production and indeed did so until after the Russo-Japanese War of 1904–5 when moored mines were shown to be a potent weapon and Britain began to produce them. Considering how much late nineteenth-century maritime strategy was bound up with attack on and defence of naval bases, it seems an extraordinary omission, even though electrically controlled mines were being constructed and were to a limited degree available. The French were almost equally backward; the Russians, Japanese and Americans were not.

TEST BEDS

Inventors flourished throughout the period. The application of previously discovered scientific principles was in full swing. All forms of heat engine and mechanical device, hydraulics, electricity and explosives were being actively exploited. The electro-magnetic spectrum was scarcely explored, the internal-combustion engine was in its infancy and the electronic computer was yet to come: but it is important to recognize how much technology there was in the Ironclad Age, and how fast the inventors were pushing it along.

In an age of such rapid material development, it was natural that extensive testing of each new device or design should take place. But testing took place in a variety of forms and environments. In France, the only country for most of the period with a naval industrial base comparable to Britain's, it was indeed centrally planned, design of hulls, propulsion and armament being vested in government agencies with the co-operation of large firms such as Creusot and Belleville. The variations and shortcomings in French material provision arose from competing (and often contradictory) doctrine on how to conduct maritime war, and from French economic and sometimes industrial weakness.

In the United States, development was spurred in the early years by the exigencies of the Civil War. There was then a lull of nearly thirty years, succeeded in the 1890s by a surge of construction in which the Bureau of Ships, aided by the emergent armament and shipbuilding firms, played a prime part. All other navies depended to a marked extent on material development in France and, even more, Britain.

British testing and trying of *matériel* was, as might have been expected, more complex and pragmatic than anywhere else. The Admiralty's part, under the Controller of the Navy, was to encourage, test and co-ordinate, the end product being whole-ship design under Admiralty control. Apart from one or two isolated

The Transatlantic Telegraph being embarked in SS Great Eastern in 1865. During the next twenty years the extension of telegraphy worldwide revolutionized the command and control of naval forces, making them far more subject to political directives from governments than previously.

units, such as Froude's testing tank and the Shoeburyness Range, there was no state-sponsored research and development establishment. Information exchange was liberal; there were remarkably few secrets, either state or commercial. This system, loose indeed by the standards of post-1945 Britain, enabled rapid progress to be made once innovation had been decided upon. And several kinds of test bed, not so much planned as naturally occurring, were available.

The first was the experience of foreign navies. As has been seen, France, the USA and Russia were often innovators in hull design, propulsion and armament; Britain's superior industrial flexibility ensured that competitors did not stay ahead for long. The technical windows remained open most often in the cases of breech-loading guns and water-tube boilers where Britain's lag was marked.

The second test bed was the British merchant shipbuilding industry. This was probably the most competitive industry in the world at the time, arguably the most competitive industry there has ever been. There was constant striving for more speed and efficiency, and unrelenting development in machinery, construction and hull form. Merchant ship practice cross-fertilized into warship construction in many areas. This in turn increased the reputation of British warship building; in 1878 an American commentator wrote: 'nearly every considerable naval power, except the US and France, has employed English [sic] designers, English shipbuilders, engineers and gun manufacturers'. This went on; in 1905 the Japanese fleet that won the battle of Tsushima (see Chapter 6), homogeneous and balanced, had been built very largely in Britain.

The third test bed was the Controller of the Navy's Department itself. Numerous trials were conducted under its sponsorship: of projectiles against armour, often on the Shoeburyness range; of torpedoes and mines, leading among other things to the invention for good or ill of torpedo-net defences; of all kinds of electrical equipment; and of the speed of new construction ships, always eagerly awaited though the sceptical pointed out the artificiality of light loading, special coal, and crack boiler and engine room staff provided by the manufacturers.

All these means of maintaining material advantage were backed by a robust institutional framework. The Institution of Naval Architects was founded in 1860, the Royal School of Naval Architecture in 1864, the Royal Corps of Naval Constructors in 1884 and the Institute of Marine Engineers in 1889. They were forums for regular discussion among naval architects and engineers and a link with the operators; many serving officers were members or attended meetings.

COMMUNICATIONS

Almost to the end of the period, communication between ships was much as it had been in Nelson's day: flag signalling supplemented by messages passed by boat and face-to-face briefing where possible. It was only after 1900 that wireless telegraphy became available, and ships out of sight of one another could communicate – at first with great difficulty – in real time.

From about 1860, however, it was possible for governments to communicate by landline (or undersea telegraph) with commanders-in-chief, provided the latter had access to a shore terminal. The strategic and operational effects, as subsequent chapters will show, were profound. Instead of months, it might now take only minutes for instructions to reach a distant command. Even if the local commander was at sea, he was likely to station a dispatch vessel at the terminal so that messages could be brought to him. As the telegraph network spread, so the level of central control was increased and the autonomy of commanders on remote stations was constrained.

OPERATIONAL CAPABILITIES

Of the five decades covered by this book, the first four were marked by technological turmoil in the three fields of warships' hull design, propulsion and armament. Often progress resembled the fabled frog's climb up the well: three jumps forward, two slips back. In the final decade, to conclude the analogy, the last three jumps took the frog clear of the well and landed it on the (fairly) level grass of the pre-dreadnought era, with the battleship–cruiser–destroyer hierarchy tidily in place and the disturbing elements of submarine and aircraft yet to come. The frog then had to work out how best to manage its new environment, a job it took ten years even partly to solve.

The operational shortcomings of the main fleets during the 1860s, and even more in the 1870s and 80s, were such that they were fortunate to go untested by major war. Ocean-fighting capacity in particular was highly suspect. The most likely outcome of an ocean campaign would have been indecisive and spasmodic encounters, frequent and embarrassing breakdowns of all descriptions, and an ineffective use of sea power. It is ironic that during these very decades, as will be seen in Chapter 3, the dogma of the decisive sea battle emerged as the centrepiece of sea power theory.

Where the new technologies did help decisively was in the operations it is now fashionable to decry, those that led to the extension of empires, notably the British but also the French, German, Russian, Japanese and American, in the Middle East, Africa, the Caribbean and East Asia. Here a multitude of riverine and amphibious operations could not have taken place without the mobility conferred by steam propulsion, the protection given by (often improvised) armour, the superiority of firepower and the control available via the telegraph system. These operations too will have their place in later chapters: but it must always be recalled that they owed their general success not only to the confidence, resource and energy displayed by the empire-builders but to the industrial strength and technical expertise of the nations they, for good or ill, represented.

CHAPTER TWO

NAVIES AND
THEIR PEOPLE

CONTINENTAL NAVIES GENERALLY much improved their organization and standards of training in the first half of the nineteenth century. The uniform and style of this French officer of the 1850s indicate the improved status and prestige of the French Navy.

NAVIES AND THEIR PEOPLE

I F TECHNOLOGY WAS advancing by leaps and bounds in the second half of the nineteenth century, the social structure and organization of the developed nations was also on the move. Navies reflected these movements. Progress was sometimes laggardly and often spasmodic; but the now generally accepted proposition, that a fighting service tends to be a microcosm of the age and nation in which it exists, held good.

ENTRY AND TRAINING

At the end of the Napoleonic Wars British sailors, and officers for that matter, were engaged, trained and organized in a way that had scarcely changed for over two hundred years. Commissioned officers were in the monarch's service and were fairly regularly paid, their low basic pay being supplemented if they were lucky by prize money. They, and the warrant officers – Master, Boatswain, Gunner – could expect pensions when they retired, if they got that far. The seamen were engaged for service in a specific ship, though in war they might be 'turned over' to another without any option. They were paid arrears of wages when the ship 'paid off' and spasmodically at other times. They too would be entitled to prize money for captures, though an individual's proportion would be far less than that of the officers. Their only pension was in the gift of the Commissioners for Greenwich Hospital.

Training was almost entirely on-the-job. There was a naval academy for young officers, but it was not compulsory to go there and it had a bad name. It was thought preferable for all – officers, volunteers and landsmen – to learn by experience at sea. Because the Royal Navy spent so much of the war years in active duty at sea, those who survived learned fast and in the most practical way.

There had, to be sure, been advances in administration in the years before 1815. The divisional system, in which a lieutenant or junior officer was placed in charge of a section of the ship's company, had come into general use in the latter part of the eighteenth century and helped to strengthen the chain of command as well as improve morale. Victualling and medical care had improved with experience and knowledge. Punishments, though still severe by later standards, were less frequent and less inclined to be inflicted for trivial offences.

Nevertheless, it was still basically a *laissez-faire* system with many opportunities for inconsistency, abuse and even fraud. And foreign navies, with one exception, followed very similar patterns. The French, for example, had a theoretically stronger recruiting system, the *Inscription Maritime*, whereby every seafarer was registered and deemed to owe a number of years' service to the state; this had some advantages over the British press-gang, even though the press accounted for a rather smaller proportion of recruits than is commonly supposed. But the French system caused almost as much resentment and evasion as the press;

and the French fleet's enforced sojourns in harbour, particularly after 1805 (the year of Trafalgar), meant that sea training fell away badly, so that it was only the very best-led and motivated ships that could take on the British on equal terms.

Much the same went for all continental navies, but it was not at all so for the United States. In the war against Britain of 1812–14 the young US Navy was manned by ardent volunteers, fit, prime seamen, well trained by enthusiastic officers and well and regularly paid. They were successful in the majority of their single-ship actions against the Royal Navy and on the Lakes. It was the numerical superiority of the British that enabled them to exert a crippling blockade on the Eastern American seaboard.

For fifteen years after the peace little changed in the personnel system. All navies were busy adjusting to severe financial and manpower stringency; it was always so after wars, but this time the reductions were dramatic. Nevertheless, in the Royal Navy at least, there was some hard thinking about entry and training, particularly of naval ratings, and this had its outcome in the institution in 1829 of a gunnery school in the hulk of the old *Excellent*. This development embodied the idea of a permanent corps of trained seamen, engaged for a fixed term to serve not in a ship but in the navy, with the possibility of re-engagement for further terms; all these ideas were quite new and laid the foundations for the structure of maritime fighting forces up to the present day.

A gun's crew at drill in 1854. Technology and technique were largely those of the previous century – the muzzle-loading gun and its furniture would have been familiar to any sailor of Nelson's day – but training had been systematized since 1830 and navies' efficiency had generally improved.

By the middle of the century the formal training of ratings had spread far beyond gunnery to seamanship generally, and it was usual for them to enter as boys, often as young as 15. The *Illustrious* at Portsmouth and *Implacable* at Devonport were the first two training ships, and instruction included knots, hitches and splices; boatwork; sail handling; elementary gunnery; cutlass and rifle drill; and the use of compass and helm. The Boy Seaman, after six months' instruction, was an embryo professional and after sea experience was able to prove himself in many a tight corner, against foul weather, the enemy, or both.

The adaptability as well as the hardihood of the trained sailor came to be more and more admired.

Parallels on the Continent were, in most cases, close. The French Navy in particular improved the quality of both its intake and its training, to the extent that in the Franco-Prussian War of 1870 the naval battalions brought ashore to fight were generally considered to have outdone the soldiers in courage and tenacity. Both Austro-Hungarian and Italian sailors in the war of 1866 showed strong fighting spirit and discipline, as did the Danes in the unequal struggle against Prussia about the same time. The Russians did not use impressment so much, however. They included a large proportion of conscripts, often of low educational standard, and while the Russian Navy was often used by other powers as a bogey to impress domestic politicians, its performance when put to the test was not expected by those in the know to be much good.

The United States Navy had learned in the hardest school of all. Up to 1860 it had been allowed to decline, under the Monroe Doctrine, into little more than a coast defence force, and the motivation of the seamen had suffered accordingly. The Civil War sharpened everything: *matériel* of course, but also initiative, fighting spirit, professional ability and teamwork. This applied almost as much to the Confederate as to the Union side, though the Confederate manpower and material base was thin and personal initiative, rather than large-scale co-ordinated effort, was prominent. From the end of the war in 1865 to the revival of the US Navy in the late 1880s, quality was maintained with difficulty, but from 1890 the service rapidly recovered its prestige and this was enhanced after the Spanish–American War (that 'splendid little war', as one American commentator called it) of 1898.

Finally, the extraordinary rise of Japan as a naval power in the 1890s owed much to the quality of the Japanese sailors and their training. This was avowedly on Western lines so far as the mechanisms of instruction went, but the spirit was strongly Japanese, spartan in the extreme to Western eyes. China was a different matter: here the Western veneer was shallower, the motivation less fierce than with the Japanese.

Many of the remarks and judgements made above apply also to officer entry and training. It steadily became more formal, instruction ashore becoming more prominent and on-the-job training beginning later. But officer entry in

Renewed pride and influence of the United States Navy are reflected, left, in this parade through the Royal Dockyard in Portsmouth, England at the turn of the century.

most navies was still by nomination until late in the nineteenth century, and though the ability to absorb instruction, and intellectual potential, were coming to the front as qualities to be sought, there was little attempt to measure them until an aspirant had served for some years. Character training, in the spirit of the British 'public' schools as typified by Dr Arnold's regime at Rugby, occupied a prominent part of the pattern in most navies, the Japanese as usual carrying Western ideas at least one step further in their singularly tough regime at Eta Jima.

The further intellectual training of officers began, in the 1870s, to be a feature. In Britain the Royal Naval College, first at Portsmouth and then at Greenwich, offered a mainly scientific course to officers of middling rank, designed to reinforce, far too early as many thought, the teaching crammed into cadets in the rigorous regime of the training ship *Britannia*; but it was for volunteers only and sea service was preferred by many. In the United States the War College and Naval Institute were founded in the 1880s, and enjoyed much less equivocal support from high authority. While in Britain a War Course was operating by 1900, there was dissatisfaction among the more thoughtful that there was too little room for discussion of the implications of the swiftly

changing naval and world scene. Years later, in 1912–13, the need for a freer and deeper exchange of views resulted in the formation of a Naval Society and the founding of its journal *The Naval Review*, with a consequent release of intellectual energy that was impressive and lasting.

A FASHIONABLE PROFESSION

One singular aspect of the naval officer corps, and it was one that affected all the major navies to an extent, was the fashionableness of the profession. Up to about 1880 most naval officers came from the same mix of the population that had supplied them for the previous four centuries: moderately educated men from middle-income families, or impecunious branches of well-off families, with a leavening of sons of 'old naval' clans with a long tradition of service, and a further seasoning of those who had worked up by sheer ability from humble beginnings. A common factor had been the desire for betterment by means of activity, ability and application.

But in the 1880s and beyond, service as a naval officer acquired a glamour that made it fashionable. It is not easy to pinpoint a single cause for such a change. No doubt the work of publicists, most of all Mahan, had something to

The training ship Britannia *in the 1890s. Officers' training was scientifically orientated and rigorous, but emphasized too strongly the absorption of facts and figures rather than encouraging leadership, initiative and intellectual skills.*

do with it; this will be more fully treated in Chapter 3. The stateliness of battle fleets, their trim appearance and their social activities – 'showing the flag' – made navies seem suddenly elegant, after the rather ramshackle appearances of the previous thirty years. The acquisition of empires, only half-conscious in previous decades, was now openly pursued and was accompanied by high-profile, rather romantic and relatively cost-free adventures. And 'Jack the Handy Man' was in the public eye; *HMS Pinafore*, Gilbert and Sullivan's sometimes ironic but always affectionate look at the navy, was first produced in 1878.

In consequence, the fleets began to be run by officers of generally higher social status than previously. Even royalty showed its interest. Certainly there had been a 'sailor king' in William IV in the early years of the century, but he had been regarded as an exception and indeed slightly eccentric. Now princely families, not confined to Britain, freely encouraged sons to pursue naval careers, royal yachts proliferated, and royal persons associated with naval officers (particularly those of 'good family') in a manner that would have been reserved for officers of the Guard in previous generations.

It is not certain whether this development was, on balance, to the benefit or the detriment of navies as a whole. Influence on their behalf was without doubt increased, to the extent that it was politically difficult, in the latter half of our period, to manage cuts in naval plans or budgets. This was most marked in Germany, where after the accession of the navalist Kaiser Wilhelm II severe pressure was brought to bear, from the top, for naval expansion. Gladstone in

The British Mediterranean Fleet in full glory in the early 1890s. The appearance of HMS Alexandra, *the white-hulled flagship, epitomizes the spit-and-polish and glamour of the era.*

Britain had resigned in protest against similar expansion some years earlier. Naturally it was not simply royal patronage that had caused these developments, but it had considerable influence. Given the latitude that generous budgets allowed, navies were able to emerge from their 'groping age' more swiftly and certainly than they would otherwise have done.

Other effects were not so beneficial. In some European navies many of the upper-class officers were dilettante in their outlook, the Russians being markedly prone to such a problem. In others, notably the French, there was a divide between the aristocratic and the more workaday officers which showed most interestingly in doctrinal differences, and these caused turmoil in naval policy in the 1880s and 90s. The German Navy, once it began its dramatic expansion in the late 1890s, was the most class-ridden of all, with anguished introspection about the family backgrounds of its officers and determined efforts to exclude those from the 'lower orders'.

In Britain the effect was more subtle, and can be summed up as a tendency to deference and conformism so well analysed by Andrew Gordon in his seminal book *The Rules of the Game*, where he traces some of the mistakes and misunderstandings at Jutland in 1916 to styles and attitudes of discipline and command stretching back at least thirty years. Privilege was more or less jealously guarded. The notion of an 'officer class' became more deeply entrenched than it had been for centuries. The result was

The navalism of Kaiser Wilhelm II was a contributory factor in the enhanced prestige of navies; other factors were the work of Mahan (whose disciple Wilhelm owned himself to be) and other naval publicists.

Promotion from the lower deck was extremely limited in all nineteenth-century navies. The most efficient and competent ratings could not expect to advance beyond Warrant Officer – a group of Gunners is pictured below – and although this carried its own status it did not satisfy the highest quality ratings.

that promotion from the lower deck to commissioned rank completely dried up for nearly the whole of the century. Warrant officers, all of whom had by definition begun their service as ratings, were in many cases highly respected (though junior ratings were quick to resent any who overplayed their status), but apart from very rare promotions for distinguished service in action there was no way up for them beyond senior warrant rank until 1903, when a limited number of promotions to Lieutenant were permitted for 'long and meritorious service'.

THE TECHNICIANS

Another complicating factor was the advent of the technician. As soon as there were engines and boilers in the fleet, there were engineers and stokers. They had quite different skills to offer. The engineer provided expertise in adjustment of his machinery, diagnosis of faults whether potential or actual, and most importantly ability to repair or improvise if something went wrong either as a result of battle damage, maloperation or fault in design. He was increasingly assisted by artificers whose training had included a long apprenticeship. The stoker, on the other hand, was expert in feeding the furnaces, physically a highly skilled job in which proper distribution of the coals over the whole grate area made all the difference between efficient and poor steaming.

It is fair to say that in no navy were these skills fully appreciated. Engineers in the Royal Navy, even the most able, struggled to gain officer status. Until 1883 only the Chief Engineer of a battleship messed in the wardroom. There is no

doubt that the social background from which most of the engineers came was regarded by other officers as inferior, and was one of the reasons for slow and overdue recognition. The institution of the Royal Naval Engineering College in the early 1880s helped to change things slowly for the better, but 'military command' still evaded the branch: that was the preserve of the seaman officer. As for the stokers, they were all ratings, recruited markedly later in life than boy seamen and more often drawn from the manufacturing areas of the country as well as from ex-soldiers and marines. Fiercely independent, they took pride in their job but formed a somewhat separate part of a ship's company.

Neither in the wardroom nor on the lower deck, therefore, was it easy to instil whole-ship consciousness. No one was more aware of this than Sir John Fisher when he became Second Sea Lord, responsible for naval personnel, in 1902. His vision was of a navy united by a common purpose, and that, he believed, could only be achieved by common training for officers. The so-called Fisher–Selborne Scheme (Lord Selborne was First Lord of the Admiralty, the political head of the Board) envisaged just such a common training, not only for seamen and engineers but for Royal Marines as well. After basic training there was to be specialization in the lower ranks, but this was to be dropped after the rank of commander when all would have equal opportunities

for further promotion. The scheme was indeed partially implemented, but the Royal Marines had strong objections, the 1914–18 War intervened to prevent its full operation, and finally in 1925 the status of engineer officers was confirmed as not amounting to 'military command' – a retrogression that was characterized then, and is still remembered, as 'the great betrayal', contrary to the ideal set two decades before.

Common training for lower-deck recruits was even more difficult to achieve. The skills required of each specialization were so different that only the most limited sort of cross-familiarization was possible, and many young ratings could not understand why even that was attempted. Once in a ship, however, some common purpose could be inculcated by various means: the performance of the ship at general drills, her achievements in sport, the smartness of the ship and her boats, and her efficiency in all-hands tasks such as coaling, were all tools in the hands of able captains, executive officers and heads of departments.

No other European navy was any more successful in absorbing the new men and their new skills than were the British. Indeed many looked to the Royal Navy as a model for their personnel structures, and though there might be differences in name and allocation of tasks, the same kinds of hierarchy prevailed and the distinction between 'military' officers and the officers of technical and specialist branches was maintained. The United States Navy was rather more innovative. They came to the notion of common training for officers somewhat before the Fisher–Selborne Scheme, and somewhat more radically; a junior officer, after his

OPPOSITE: Admiral 'Jacky' Fisher, as Second Sea Lord in 1903, initiated the Fisher–Selborne Scheme aimed at 'up to a certain point some community of knowledge and a lifelong community of sentiment'. This was to give all officers – Seamen, Engineers and Royal Marines – common training and equal promotion prospects. The scheme was effectively ditched in the 1920s.

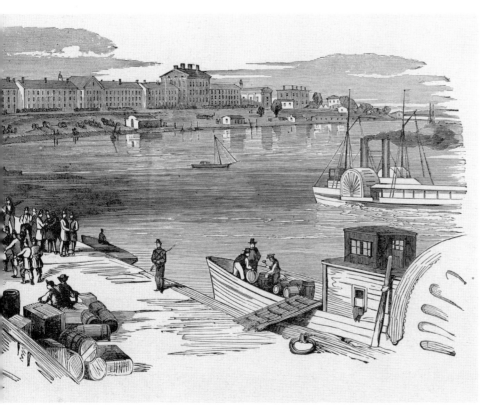

The US Naval Academy at Annapolis instituted a broad, scientifically based course at a relatively late starting age, followed by a broad spectrum of appointments in an officer's early career, so that a 'deck' billet was likely to be followed by an engineering appointment.

training at the Naval Academy, might find himself as a ship's engineer in one appointment and a gunnery officer and bridge watch-keeper in the next. The consequence was an officer corps that was technically orientated, with a broad base of experience; the obverse of the coin was that inevitably the expertise was rather thinly spread, so that the officer relied more heavily on the senior enlisted men in his department than would the more specialized British officer. However, given the generally high level of technical resource and adaptability available in the United States' population as a whole, the system worked well.

One thing the new technical men brought with them to all navies has perhaps been consistently underestimated as a factor: coal.

'Coal Ship' was an all-hands operation, an 'evolution' in nautical terms, which tested ships' organization and spirit to the limit. After the bunkers had been filled everyone had to turn to and clean up. This might occur weekly at times of intensive operation.

Coal was pervasive in every sense. Major warships carried 1,000 tons, on average, in their bunkers. The embarkation of such quantities, every time the ship needed refuelling – as often as once a week when on sea service – involved the whole ship's company in arduous and very dirty work. It was an all-hands task to test ship spirit, to be sure, but the mess needed to be cleaned up afterwards. Moreover, steaming – and particularly high-speed steaming – caused smoke, however expertly fired were the boilers. The optimum funnel emission was a 'light brown haze' and this was perhaps tolerable, but all too often it was supplanted by a black and horrible cloud. However carefully chosen the ship's course relative to the wind, some smuts would land on the deck.

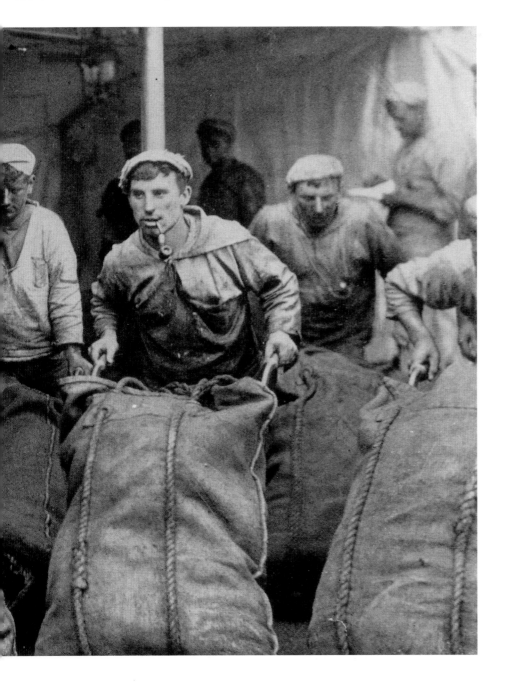

During the 1860s and up to the mid 1880s the effects of coal throughout the ships of all fleets appear to have met with what might be called grumbling acceptance. Steam, after all, had its conveniences, even though what produced it was mucky and its purveyors – the engineers and stokers – were never absolutely clean and tidy and sailorlike. Moreover, in most ships of that period it was always possible to shut down the engines and proceed under sail, provided the wind was

Queen Victoria's Diamond Jubilee Review in 1897 was an occasion for a display not only of loyalty by her Fleet but of its latent power and acknowledged influence. The reputation of the 'British Tar' was at its peak.

not in the wrong direction and operational necessity did not demand steaming.

But from that time onwards, the reaction became sharper. For one thing, more and more ships had no sailing rig at all; steaming was their only mode of progress. For another, the increasing social standing of navies meant that the outward appearance of their ships had, in the view of many, to be dignified and attractive beyond any possible reproach. Finally, in the Royal Navy at any rate, a long tradition of scrupulous cleanliness – instituted mainly for health reasons well over a hundred years before – was felt to have been undermined and to require reinstatement.

GLISTENING FLEETS

The result was an obsession with smartness and surface glitter that reached its zenith in the 1890s in the British Mediterranean Fleet, though its influence spread far and wide through all navies and decades forward in time. (The author believes his hands to have been among the last to holystone a wooden deck in the training cruiser, well after the Second World War.) Brightwork gleamed, paint was applied so liberally that ships lay appreciably lower in the water than they were designed to do, and Admiral 'Pompo' Heneage wore white gloves for inspections, replaced as necessary from a spare stock carried on a salver by his coxswain. After each coaling every nook and cranny was scoured clean of coal, every man likewise.

Any navy putting such emphasis on outward appearance was unlikely to be at tip-top fighting efficiency, and so events – though not the critical event of battle – went to prove. Main armaments were fired rarely and then under artificial conditions; the British Mediterranean Fleet's annual 'gunlayers' test' in 1899 consisted of single-gun firing at a stationary target, at a range of less than a mile, with the firing ship on a steady course and speed. The arrival of 'Jacky' Fisher as Commander-in-Chief, and the innovations of Percy Scott the gunnery specialist, improved matters as the century turned, but performance did not match potential for years.

Nor were other navies in better case, with some exceptions. These were the Japanese, spurred by feelings of injustice and ambition to redress wrongs, in particular those done by Russia; the Americans, who had conducted effective operations – admittedly against a much weaker and exhausted opponent – in 1898; and the growing German Navy, with the advantages of youth, ambition and a burgeoning industrial base on its side. All, to be sure, were far inferior in numbers to the Royal Navy, which could still bask in the sunlight of its perceived superiority.

Nor were the effects of the 'spit and polish' era all detrimental. Sailors were earnest, hard-working, tough and self-reliant as never before. Their pride in their own ship, in their fleet and in their navy, has seldom been surpassed. With pride came confidence: in the naval college at Osborne, opened in 1904, the first notice a cadet saw was 'There is nothing the Royal Navy cannot do' and, as will be seen in later chapters, that reflected much of the performance of the previous decades and the spirit that carried the service into the First World War. But that confidence was replicated in many other naval services round the world. Navies had acquired prestige.

A legend in his lifetime, Admiral 'Pompo' Heneage terrified officers and ratings with his zero-tolerance of dirt, slovenly dress and incorrect ceremonial.

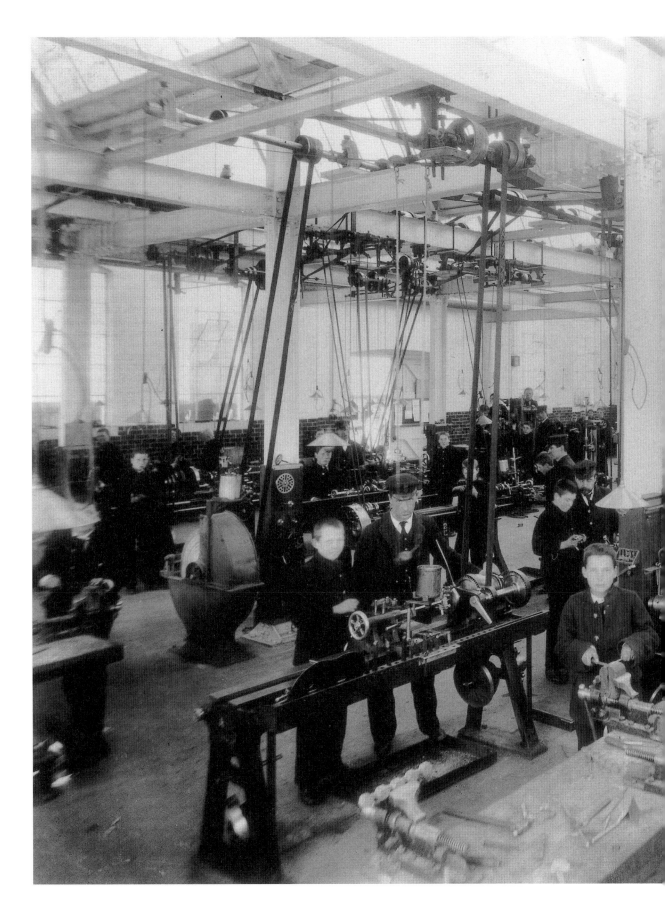

A metalworking class at the workshops of the Royal Naval College in the early 1900s. Boys were entered as Cadets at the age of about 12$\frac{1}{2}$ and went to sea as midshipmen at about 16.

CHAPTER THREE

THEORIES OF SEA WARFARE

HORATIO LORD NELSON *was, for most of the publicists of the day, the epitome of naval strategist, tactician and leader. His offensive spirit, courage and sense of duty were emphasized, his imagination and unconventionality sometimes less so. His shortcomings were ignored or explained.*

THEORIES OF SEA WARFARE

'WHEN IT HAS NOTHING else to do,' a wise Director of Naval Plans said in 1967, 'the Ministry of Defence reorganizes itself.' A hundred years before, he might have paraphrased it in a slightly different context: When there is no sea warfare, theorists of sea warfare theorize.

BRITISH THEORY

It might have been expected that such intellectual enquiry would begin across the Channel; after all, French theorists such as Hoste in the early eighteenth century, and Morogues fifty years later, had made theoretical studies of sea warfare well in advance of comparable systematic treatment by any British author. Or, perhaps, it could have come from across the Atlantic, in the wake of the bloody strife that ended in 1865 and in the form of 'lessons learnt'.

Surprisingly, in view of the well-known British leaning towards action rather than words and pragmatism rather than theory, the first discussion came from neither France nor America, but from Britain itself. The Colomb brothers, first of the overt publicists, were both officers in the sea service. Philip, the elder, was in the navy, reaching the rank of Vice Admiral, and had a varied career of active service; his first book, published in 1873, was called *Slave Catching in the Indian Ocean*. John, born six years later, was in the Royal Marine Artillery but retired at the age of 31 and entered Parliament, where he served for over twenty years.

Philip H. Colomb as a Vice Admiral. With his brother John he was one of the first naval publicists of the Ironclad Age. He adopted an approach based on the history of sailing navies and advocated an uncompromising strategy based upon command of the sea. His views on tactical manoeuvres were equally rigid.

While both the Colombs were passionately interested in naval power generally and Britain's naval supremacy in particular, they took quite different approaches. John was in essence a publicist of what a hundred years later would have been called 'The Naval Case'. He addressed contemporary issues without seeking to draw many lessons from history. He had some reason for this approach: a Royal Commission of 1859–60 had addressed questions of naval defence from precisely the standpoint that the advent of steam had created a quite new strategic situation, and concluded that the security of bases was of paramount importance. It was indeed the theoretical basis for the construction of extensive forts along the south coast, still in many cases extant and known to most as 'Palmerston's Follies'. John Colomb took issue with these ideas in his pamphlet 'The Protection of our Commerce, and Distribution of our War Forces Considered' (1867), arguing that sea communications were the basis of maritime strategy and that a strong force in the English Channel could protect the focus of British sea communications and also control the logical route for either invasion or an assault on bases.

Philip Colomb, much influenced by the magisterial figure of John Knox Laughton, a naval instructor with a rigorous 'scientific' approach to naval topics, took a more historical and analytical line, while according priority to John whose work, he much later wrote, was 'the keynote to all … subsequent discussions'. Philip was concerned to extract the eternal verities of sea power from a study of history. In doing so he formulated – not, he added, without agonized consideration – the doctrine that command of the sea was the only rational aspiration for a maritime strategy. Nothing less would be satisfactory; a disputed command would be insufficient to ensure sea communications or project power abroad. 'The frontier of our Empire', he wrote, 'is the enemy's coast line.'

Philip Colomb's theories had perforce to be based on the only history available, and that was overwhelmingly the history of sailing-ship warfare. Without doubt his deductions from the later phases of the Napoleonic Wars, when Britain had got closer to command of the sea than ever before, were as valid as any derived from a particular case; and they were palatable to a navy that wished to hold a pre-eminent position, and a public that wanted it so.

THE *JEUNE ÉCOLE*

But it could not be expected that they would pass unchallenged across the Channel. France in the days of Napoleon III had chafed at British naval preponderance, and indeed in the late 1850s and early 1860s had mounted a significant challenge, soon extinguished by superior British industrial strength. In the early 1870s, however, new thought in France formulated a set of ideas founded in the potential of the most up-to-date technology. It was a strategy specifically for the weaker naval power. This was the *Jeune École*.

The forerunner of this school was Baron Richard Grivel whose *De la Guerre Maritime* was published in 1869, but its leader is generally held to have been Rear Admiral Théophile Aube, ably backed by the writing of several other commentators such as Gabriel Charmes and J. H. Vignot. Taking as their departure point the advent of new weapons, in particular the torpedo and the mine, but looking forward also to the submarine, they argued that the reign of battleships was over; blockade was no longer sustainable; enemy seaborne commerce was therefore vulnerable. Aube in particular argued that the laws of war, as embodied in the 1856 Treaty of Paris, would quickly become unworkable in a major conflict, and that ruthless attacks on enemy commerce would be widespread.

Unlike many radical thinkers, Aube had an opportunity to put his ideas into practice, for in 1886 he became Minister of Marine; and unlike most radical thinkers who achieved office, he did not compromise when faced with the realities of administration and finance. He cancelled battleship building programmes, ordered very large numbers of torpedo boats and fast cruisers, and fostered submarine development.

As has already been suggested, technology was not ready for the realization of Aube's theories. The torpedo boats at that stage of development were suitable only for harbour work; ideas of carrying them in motherships to remote areas were never realized; the cruisers were subject to technical and, even more stringently, logistic constraints; a viable propulsion system for submarines was not yet available. Moreover, French politics were volatile, and in the event Aube lasted no more than eighteen months as Minister of Marine.

He was succeeded by a more conservative succession of Ministers and a corps of senior officers who favoured the much more traditional school of *La Grande Guerre*. This called for balanced fleets based upon battleships, and was the line taken by the more mainstream and aristocratic officers. Some of the measures set up by Aube remained in place, notably in submarine development where France led the world for the next decade, but in general there was a return to conventional force structures. Aube remains, however, a prophet. His greatest contribution can be encapsulated in a very simple statement about the future of sea warfare: like would not necessarily fight like any more. In hindsight, that is a blinding glimpse of the obvious. It was not at all so at the time.

The most influential naval publicist of the Ironclad Age, and probably of all time, Alfred Thayer Mahan made his name with The Influence of Sea Power upon History *(1890) and followed with other impressive historical analysis. He believed in the necessity of eliminating an opposing fleet in decisive battle so that sea power could subsequently be exercised.*

LUCE AND MAHAN

Meanwhile, across the Atlantic, intellects were stirring. The foundation of the US Naval War College under Captain (subsequently Admiral) Stephen B. Luce in the mid 1880s was, in retrospect, a seminal event. The United States had had twenty years to recover from its civil war, years when it had been preoccupied not only with reconciliation and reconstitution of the Union, but exceptionally rapid expansion and development of the continent. An oceanic navy had been low on the nation's list of priorities. Now, however, eyes were beginning to turn outwards.

Luce was prominent among those taking this view. He looked for assistants who could help in forming a vision for the future and lighted upon Alfred Thayer Mahan. Mahan was at first sight an unlikely candidate: an officer, by then a captain, who disliked sea service, was unclubbable and not highly regarded by his fellows. But he was painstaking, industrious and had already published work on the Civil War that Luce regarded as promising. In 1885 Mahan was asked to take up the post of lecturer at the War College, and accepted at once.

It was during his preparation for the post that his ability to penetrate a mass of evidence to reach fundamental principles began to show itself. It is said that his idea of the immense influence that sea power could exert, far beyond the simple impact of a tactical situation, stemmed from a study of Roman strategy during the Punic Wars, and it is significant that his first major work does begin with that very topic. Certainly, by the time he started to lecture at the War College in 1886, his core theories were already well formulated.

He first reached a wider public in *The Influence of Sea Power upon History*, published in 1890. Mahan's approach in this book, probably the most influential work on the subject before or since, was as historical as Philip Colomb's and was as much, if not more, influenced by the methods of Laughton whom he knew and respected. In this book he covered only the period from 1660 to the end of the American War of Independence in 1783. That time was in general one of British naval supremacy, but that was no problem for Mahan who had great admiration for Britain. Indeed, he adopted Britain as an archetype of the successful maritime nation: favoured by geography, in size, conformation and position, possessing a hardy population stock bred to the sea, with an outward-looking and commercially enterprising government. Given these qualities, Mahan argued, a country was most likely to succeed in trading and colonial enterprises and to be able to protect its ventures by means of a powerful navy. Britain had done just that.

Mahan thus sought to extract the eternal verities of sea power from the history of wars that involved only sailing navies, just as Philip Colomb did. His work was subtler and wider-ranging, into economic and political fields, but its approach was essentially similar. This applied too to his later work which appeared in 1892 on *The Influence of Sea Power on the French Revolution and Empire*. Here, inevitably, Mahan fell under the spell of Nelson, whom he regarded as the embodiment and ultimate practitioner of the principles Mahan had later formulated, and in 1899 he published a *Life of Nelson*.

It is no exaggeration to say that Mahan's writings had a worldwide impact that changed the shape of armaments for a generation, and thinking about strategy for much longer than that. There was, from 1890 to 1914, far more emphasis than hitherto on naval forces and particularly on battle fleets, which Mahan regarded as the only true basis for naval power. In political terms, his work had been directed principally towards the US government, and it fell there upon receptive ears to the extent that the already tentatively begun building programme was swiftly accelerated. But it was also seized upon by governments across the Atlantic. In Britain the navalists quoted it as justification of all their aspirations and fears, and rode on it to naval expansion. In France, Italy and Russia the proponents of large and balanced fleets made use of its theories and achieved increases in naval budgets accordingly. But it was in Germany that the influence was greatest. The relatively new and ambitious Kaiser Wilhelm II was so impressed that he was said to sleep with a copy of Mahan under his pillow, and he certainly read it from cover to cover.

*Grand Admiral Alfred von
Tirpitz, selected by Kaiser
Wilhelm II to develop the
Imperial German Navy in
1897. He founded the
concept of a 'Risk Fleet'
which would pose to the
Royal Navy a threat of
unacceptable damage and
thereby free Germany for
colonial expansion.*

KAISER WILHELM II AND TIRPITZ

But the naval legacy that Wilhelm had inherited was a relatively small one. Germany had a rapidly expanding industrial base, its armament industry for land forces was formidable as had been shown by the Franco-Prussian War, and it had good armament and armour-producing plant at Krupp. But there was a great deal of ground to be made up if any challenge was to be mounted to the pre-eminent Royal Navy, and this became a notion embedded in the Kaiser's mind.

In 1897 he selected as Secretary of State in the Reich Navy Office a man who would, he hoped, solve the problem. Alfred von Tirpitz was a naval officer of fertile mind, wide influence and much organizational skill, and as suggested in the previous paragraph he had some industrial assets to work with as well as a keen and active officer corps. But he was beginning from a very low force level in the navy itself.

Tirpitz formulated a daring strategy specifically directed against Britain, and it was this which dominated the arms race that ensued and was only one third of the way through when the period of this book ends. The strategy was called significantly the *Risikogedanke* and the High Seas Fleet that emerged was a *Risikflotte*. The theory went like this. Even if the German Navy was never numerically equal to the Royal Navy, it could be constructed and organized so

that it would be able to inflict damage on the British fleet (or, preferably, isolated parts of it), which Britain with all her other preoccupations would find unacceptable. Therefore, Britain would not willingly take on Germany in any war which threatened the British fleet in this way. Therefore, Britain would perforce have to concede to Germany the opportunity for colonial expansion and continental influence which the Kaiser desired: a place in the sun.

The out-turn of Tirpitz's strategy falls outside the period of this book, but it is worth noting that neither on the small scale – the Agadir Crisis of 1911 – nor the grand – the Great War of 1914–18 – did it work as planned. This was because Britain's response was in both building and deployment terms more robust and radical than Tirpitz had bargained for; her fleet was maintained in large numbers and at high quality, and concentrated in home waters to the extent that it always outnumbered the German High Seas Fleet by a considerable margin, a margin that enabled detachments to be made to neutralize German distant-water forays and to resist successfully any attempt to defeat it in detail.

Thus by the end of the century there was a growing orthodoxy in sea power theory based upon the work of the Colombs and Mahan and backed by writers in other countries whose work in hindsight looks derivative but was no doubt well received at the time. This orthodoxy, which included the *Grande Guerre* school in

The German Brandenburg Squadron comprising pre-dreadnoughts at the turn of the century. The exceptionally rapid mobilization of Germany's great industrial strength to produce a powerful navy triggered an arms race that continued to the outbreak of the First World War.

Experimental submarines began to be built in the 1870s and by the late 1880s France, the USA and (with reluctance) Britain all had craft that could, in theory and sometimes in practice, submerge at will.

France, held that sea power with all its strategic and economic benefits was conferred by command of the sea, and that such command could be achieved by the defeat of the opponent's main force in a decisive battle or battles. It was a simple concept favouring the stronger naval power, and as such highly acceptable to the British who were at the time pre-eminent, and to the Americans who aspired to that status.

The only serious challenges to orthodox theory had come from the *Jeune École*, now discredited mainly because the attempted realization of its aspirations had failed to happen, and the emerging strategy of Tirpitz, which was quite different from that of the *Jeune École* but was, equally, a strategy founded upon the aspirations of the weaker naval power. Neither was given much credit by the Anglo-Saxons or their followers. Nevertheless, some commentators were beginning to suggest that the orthodox theory was perhaps a trifle over-simple.

Of these the most prominent was Sir Julian Corbett, a barrister by training and historian by inclination, who began to publish in 1898 and became a lecturer at the Royal Naval War College at Greenwich in 1902. His historical studies had convinced him that the exercise of sea power was a more complex and subtle business than simply bashing the daylights out of the opposing battle fleet and then exerting a stranglehold on enemy commerce while pursuing one's own. For

one thing, it might not be achievable by that means if the enemy avoided battle while remaining a potential menace. For another, its application once command was achieved, by whatever means, covered wider issues including, critically, the support of continental alliances by combined operations mounted from the sea. Finally, Corbett accepted that sea warfare had limitations: it was unlikely by itself to win wars outright, and if in special circumstances it did, the process would be long and arduous.

Corbett's thinking was a good deal too subtle and complex for many of the orthodox persuasion. They preferred to keep it simple, and indeed most did so, from Sir David Beatty downwards, throughout the First World War and beyond. As a footnote, Corbett was the official historian of the naval side of the First World War, but his work was not entirely appreciated by the Admiralty, who in the third volume inserted a disclaimer to the effect that they disagreed with Corbett's 'tendency to minimize the importance of seeking battle and forcing it to a conclusion'. That was written in 1923, but it reflected a long official unease at some of Corbett's thinking.

There were two emerging elements of sea warfare that, in hindsight, were not sufficiently addressed by any of the theorists – even Aube, though he got closest. These were the submarine and the aircraft.

By 1900 submarines with clear operational capability were beginning to be built. Thereafter the evolution of the submarine as a war vessel was extraordinarily rapid, so that by the outbreak of the First World War it was already a formidable sea-denial vehicle.

It is not always realized that these two developments were in fact nearly two decades apart in time. The first viable submarines, designed by Philip Garratt in Britain, Gustave Zédé in France, and John Holland in America, all submerged (and, sometimes, resurfaced) at about the same time, in the late 1880s. The first powered flight was not made until 1904, and though the author is reluctant to dismiss the air element until it peeps out at the very end of this book, it has to be admitted that it does not belong to the Ironclad Age.

Consciousness of the potential of the submarine was however well within our period. But it was limited by the imagination, or lack of it, displayed by those who knew and thought about it. Fisher was in no doubt that it would change the face of sea warfare, but tended to regard it as a potential adjunct to fleets rather than a lone predator. Sir Arthur Wilson, though his reaction sounded Blimpish ('underhand ... and damned un-English ... treat all submarines as pirates in wartime ... and hang all the crews'), probably predicted more accurately what was going to happen under the stress of war. Tirpitz, interestingly, discouraged submarine development to the extent of retarding the careers of its proponents, revealing himself as essentially a big-navy man.

The pundits, on the whole, displayed less imagination than the practitioners. The Colombs, Mahan and even Corbett paid scant attention to the submarine's potential. This stemmed partly from their overwhelmingly historical approach, drawn perforce from the experience of mainly sailing navies before the rapid and unprecedented developments of the previous thirty or forty years. It also stemmed from a belief that the rule of law would extend to the conduct of war at sea; attacks on commerce would be governed by the laws of capture, as modified by the Declaration of Paris of 1856 which abolished privateering, and the ideas of sinking at sight or not making proper provision for the safety of crews were not admissible. The downfall of Aube, with his much harsher ideas, was probably a comfort to the more orthodox. At all events, questions of commerce protection revolved almost entirely round the threat of surface raiders rather than that of submarines. It was understandable; there had been experience, as later chapters will show, of effective surface-ship actions against commerce since the advent of steam, while submarines were as yet evidently incapable of conducting similar campaigns. The necessary leap of imagination, for most of the pundits, was just not there.

Ships in Barry Dock in the 1890s. The immensely large and heterogeneous British merchant fleet was at once an instrument of trade and expansion, a powerful economic asset, and a potential vulnerability, during the Ironclad Age.

PATROLLING STATIONS AND TRADE ROUTES C. 1885

This map is an amalgam of two contemporary documents and illustrates British concepts of trade protection in the last quarter of the nineteenth century. Convoy was not considered an option, and a system of patrol and 'hunting' was substituted.

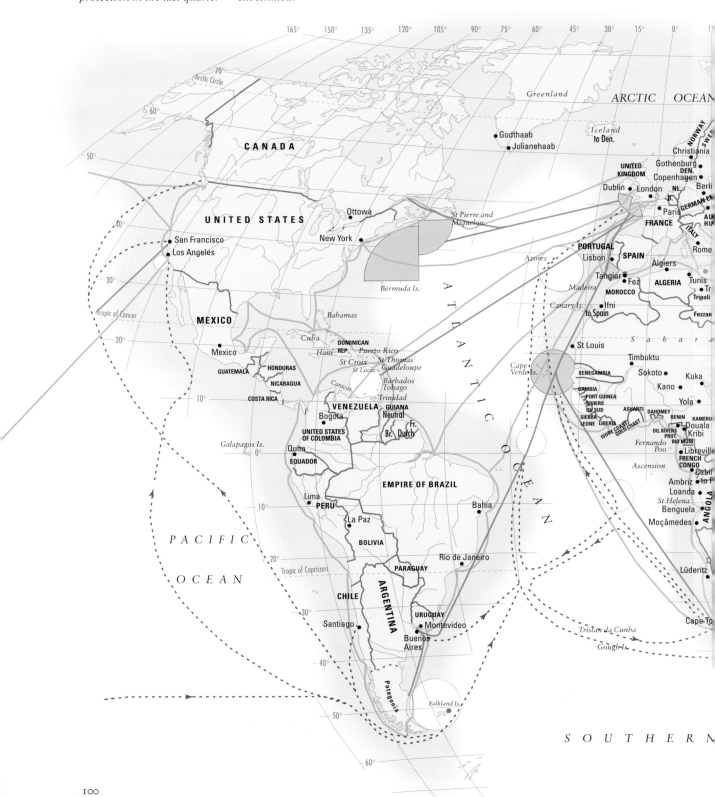

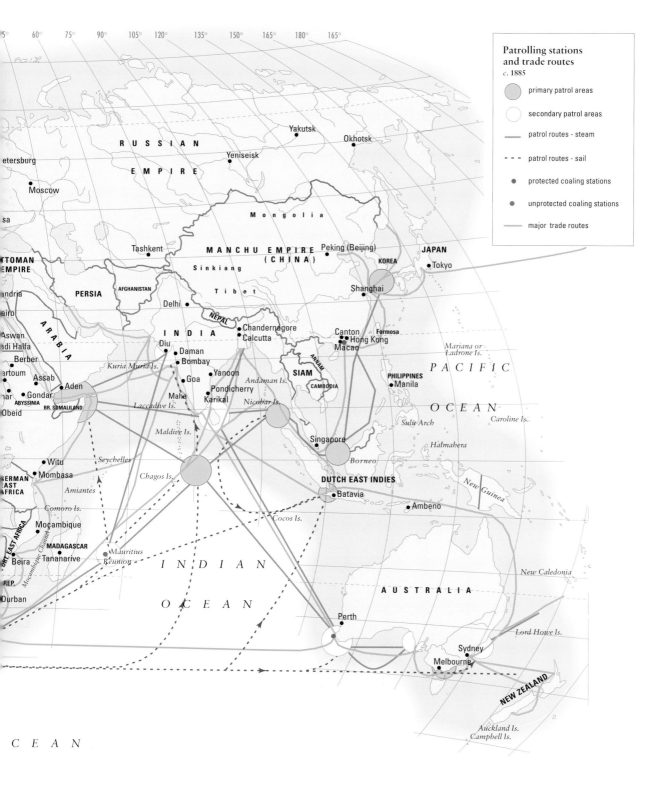

Patrolling stations
and trade routes
c. 1885

- primary patrol areas
- secondary patrol areas
— patrol routes - steam
- - - patrol routes - sail
● protected coaling stations
● unprotected coaling stations
— major trade routes

TRADE PROTECTION

Commerce protection, indeed, was a preoccupation of the theorists during the last years of the century. It was most acutely felt in Britain. With a trading fleet four times as large as any other nation, an overseas empire of greater extent than any other and a population dependent on imports for about half its food needs, let alone raw materials for its industry, Britain was vulnerable. The unpleasant sight of competitors building fast cruisers apparently suitable for commerce raiding was certainly one of the spurs to the campaign of the navalists in the mid 1880s.

The classical answer, formulated by Mahan above all others but echoed by many, was that command of the sea, achieved by decisive battle, would enable the victorious fleet so to dominate the ocean as to drive away the majority of potential raiders. There would always be some craft of the enemy to conduct a *guerre de course*, but in history this had never been a successful strategy and there was no reason why it should be different in modern conditions. This general theory was reinforced by studies within the British Admiralty and Foreign Intelligence Committee which estimated that raiders could do most damage at

the focal points of trade and that if British forces, working of course from a basis of general dominance, were concentrated in these areas the threats could be contained if not eliminated.

Convoy was not considered a necessary measure. The escort by warships of formed bodies of merchantmen, which had proved so effective as a means of maintaining sea traffic for several centuries, was thought not to be appropriate to the age of steam, free trade and highly networked maritime institutions. Commercial firms, sensitive to the pressures of supply and demand, would not tolerate the delays that convoy imposed. Moreover, many in naval circles thought convoy too defensive a measure to be consistent with the notion of sea command on which naval strategy was founded. Much more acceptable were the images of the hunting field, where predators were to be searched for, flushed out and driven away or destroyed.

It is argued by some historians that at the time these policies were formulated, they were in fact appropriate. The threat was not then the submarine but the much more visible cruiser or auxiliary surface raider. These were not likely to do significant damage in the open oceans, however closely defined the

Convoy was the customary means of protecting merchant ships, proved in previous wars and subsequent ones (as, here, in 1918). It was discounted during the Ironclad Age for technical and economic reasons. Its rejection fortunately was not put to the test.

'imperial sea lanes' might be, but to be effective must concentrate in focal areas; and there, with the great assistance of the newly installed worldwide telegraph system, those in command of the covering forces could deploy such forces to bring them to book. A convoy policy would have meant an entirely different force structure and organization, and it is not even certain whether effective convoy escorts could have been constructed given the existing technology.

While these arguments are respectable, they fail to explain why for a relatively brief period – say at most forty years – convoy should have been a less effective method of commerce protection than patrolling and hunting, while before and after that time it was proved to have been the correct policy. The virtues of convoy – concentration of targets so that raiders' searches for them were more difficult and hazardous, and protection of those targets so that actual attacks on them gave the protectors a good chance of destroying the attacker – were no less during this period, and though the organization of a convoy system was not in accord with the laissez-faire spirit of the time, it would have been accepted as a necessity as soon as it became apparent that adopting a convoy formation would diminish losses. This had been so in 1793–1815 and was so again in 1917. It is curious that it should be regarded as invalid for 1885.

IMPERIAL DEFENCE

Another form of vulnerability peculiar to Britain was that of her Empire. It was unique for the period because it was so much more mature than any other; the control of the Indian subcontinent and settlement of Canada and Australia were well established by 1860, and for the rest of the century, when other European

The battle-cruiser HMAS Australia. While navies for the larger British dominions were instituted at the turn of the century, doctrine insisted that the prime defence of the Empire rested with the main British battle fleet.

states and the USA were busy acquiring colonial possessions, Britain was expanding and consolidating from an already established base. But there was a downside to this: great possessions entailed great security responsibilities. Moreover, the emerging dominions were not only conscious of their vulnerability but keen to have some autonomy in their own defence without, however, having to devote too many of their local resources to it.

The question was a considerable preoccupation for the British Government from 1887 onwards, when at the Colonial Conference it was agreed that a trade protection squadron for Australian and New Zealand waters should be formed, partly funded by subventions from those dominions themselves. In the early 1900s this agreement was temporarily renewed, but by then it was becoming clear that Australia, New Zealand and Canada would soon be forming their own naval forces, and these emerged in the years immediately preceding the First World War.

However, Britain insisted that the core of imperial defence should remain the Royal Navy, following the established principle that a dominant battle fleet should ensure command of the sea and therefore secure the Empire. This proposition was not made any more palatable to the far-flung dominions by the concentration of the British battle fleet in home waters to meet the German threat, but they had to accept it and indeed several major units of that fleet were financed by the dominions and colonies. The politics of this situation in the last two decades of the Ironclad Age were not easy and indeed remained fraught for many decades after it, to the extent that there was a strong sense of betrayal in Australia at the perceived inadequacy of Britain's response to the Japanese threat in 1941.

As has been suggested, no other colonial power had comparable problems. The French, Dutch, German and latterly American empires were very largely recent acquisitions and no major emerging settler nations were involved. Naval forces required for security were of a quite different order from those of Britain – mainly patrol and river craft with a stiffening of cruisers – and control of deployment and policy rested with metropolitan centres. Once more it is difficult to overstate the importance of the telegraph; local commanders were now in more or less constant touch with their capitals, where earlier in the nineteenth century they would have had to act on their own initiative.

So much for the theories and politics of sea power in the Ironclad Age. What of the tactics that were to put theory into practice?

TACTICAL THEORY

It was clear from the early days of steam power that manoeuvres designed to bring ships into action could potentially be made more precise and certain than they had been under sail alone. Movement in the required direction, and alterations of course and speed, were not only more likely to be achieved but could be predicted by experimental data; ships' turning circles were known, and the number of revolutions per minute that their screws were ordered to make –

readily adjusted by the engineers on the throttles – regulated their speed. Thus the difficulties of getting a fleet into nearly simultaneous action, that had bedevilled sailing navies through previous centuries and helped to produce such débâcles as Toulon in 1744 and Minorca in 1756, could in theory be minimized by the miracle of steam.

But even when the complexities of steam-with-sail had dropped away, by about 1875, the handling of a large fleet under steam alone did present problems. Simple formations such as the single line could be unwieldy, causing great station-keeping difficulty for the rearmost ships, and inappropriate too when a more compact formation was required. But more complex formations were difficult to alter without elaborate manoeuvring or radical alterations of course and speed by some of the ships involved.

STEAM TACTICS

'Steam tactics', the means of manoeuvring steam-powered naval forces in peace and war, were an obsession of navies in the Ironclad Age. They maintain their fascination, as is shown in these sets of diagrams, published nearly 100 years apart, which attempt to analyse the Victoria–Camperdown collision in 1893. The figures are reproduced without any of the accompanying text, simply to indicate the conundrums that become apparent when such manoeuvres go wrong. Readers who require further argument should refer to the sources themselves.

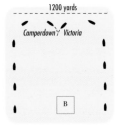

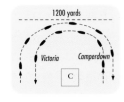

MANOEUVRES – I

ABOVE: *This analysis shows how Sir George Tryon had stationed his leading ships too close together, so that their turn inwards must, if done with*

normal manoeuvring helm, result in collision; adjustment as in A (radical tightening of the turn), or C (both ships under very easy wheel) would have

been needed for safety. Source: *Sir William Laird Clowes,* The Royal Navy: A History from the Earliest Times to 1900 *(Sampson Low, 1903).*

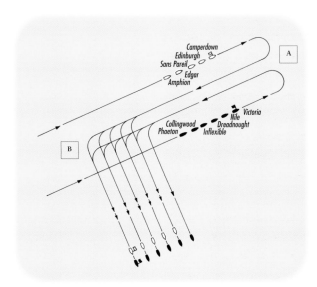

A	1st Division, turn in succession, 16 points to port. 2nd Division, turn in succession, 16 points to starboard.
B	All ships turn together 8 points to port.

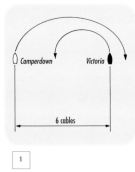

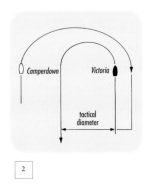

MANOEUVRES – II AND III

LEFT: *This diagram shows Sir George Tryon's assumed anchorage plan on 22 June 1893. This would have been a perfectly safe plan if columns had started 10 cables apart. Since they were 6 cables apart, it was fatal.*

ABOVE: *Many theories have been advanced as to Tryon's intentions, the most popular being shown here. But if that was his plan, he did not make it clear.* Source: *Andrew Gordon,* The Rules of the Game *(John Murray, 1996).*

These difficulties were addressed by the Royal Navy in great (almost certainly excessive) detail in the late 1870s and throughout the 1880s. The Mediterranean Fleet under Admiral Sir Geoffrey Phipps Hornby took great pride in its elaborate demonstration of 'steam tactics', and its tight control was never better shown than in the deterrent passage of the Dardanelles in 1878. This was expressly designed to impress foreigners, and did. Moreover, Phipps Hornby, though a great practitioner of the set piece, was also a clear-thinking leader and had he been called upon to go to war he would almost certainly have found a way out of elaboration into the simplicity required for battle, even with the heterogeneous force at his command.

It was not so with lesser commanders. During the 1880s manoeuvres became ever more complicated, signals proliferated and the more radical officers in the fleet complained – in private – of 'goose-stepping' exercises involving enormous displays of bunting that had less and less relevance to the business of getting a fleet into action. As Andrew Gordon has rightly written, product was subordinated to process; the end was forgotten, the means were everything. The revised signal book of 1889 was in two volumes and had over 500 pages.

An attempt to cut through the flummery and return to first principles was made by Sir George Tryon when he became Commander-in-Chief in the Mediterranean in 1891. A man of fertile mind and dominating personality, he instituted a system of simple signals that were designed for use in action, when smoke might obscure visibility and signal halyards be shot away. The fleet, and most other flag officers, reacted with relief, though there were some who believed they could work the old system even in action. But Tryon tragically died when his flagship *Victoria* was rammed by the *Camperdown* on 22 June 1893. The bitter irony was that the collision occurred not during one of Tryon's free battle manoeuvres, but in a formal set-piece alteration of formation; and that it was due almost certainly to a simple aberration of mind, stubbornly persisted in, by Tryon himself. He was heard to say after the disaster, and before he went down with his flagship, 'It is all my fault.'

However irrelevant the disaster might be in assessing the validity of Tryon's theories for battle manoeuvres, it did in fact serve to discredit them, and the Royal Navy reverted to its previous formalism. The tension between the two ways of handling a fleet – which was much older than steam, and persisted well after the First World War – was resolved temporarily in favour of deference and obedience to rigid control.

One further question the Royal Navy had to answer was not resolved until right at the end of the Ironclad period: at what range did it intend to fight?

It is fair to say that many senior officers did address this question in the later decades of the nineteenth century. Their overwhelming consensus appears to have been 'as near point blank as possible'. That was not founded simply on Nelsonian memories. The fact was that guns were not very accurate, rates of fire were slow (often even slower than those of line-of-battle ships of sailing days) and

Admiral Sir Percy Scott, a great innovator in the gunnery field and iconoclast against the 'spit-and-polish' school. The existence of a well-distributed 'Spy' cartoon of this officer, who was raised to the baronetcy but never commanded a fleet, indicates the high image of the Royal Navy during the Edwardian era.

armour known to be resistant at long ranges. Moreover, the ram, that instrument of Victorian machismo, was regarded as an available weapon.

In consequence, until about 1900 the gunlayers' test, as was earlier stated, was conducted at ranges far below the maximum effective range of the guns and in highly artificial conditions, and at that range accuracy was not even particularly good. Guns were very seldom fired in anything like action conditions, and many captains – egged on by their executive officers, who had a vested interest in keeping the ship shiny – were reluctant to conduct practice firings at all.

The ethos began to change as the century turned. Captain, later Admiral, Percy Scott was the leader in what amounted to a revolution. He invented devices that improved accuracy, he advocated and carried through changes to firing practices that used much more of the guns' range potential. He was a figure of controversy in the spit-and-polish navy, but to him must be given much of the credit for the advances in gunnery that made the British fleet such a formidable force by 1905.

Of other European navies, only the French studied tactics systematically throughout the period. Their organization included a Squadron of Evolutions which tested, to the extent possible, ideas put forward by the high command. Their main problem was, as in so many other things, that performance did not match aspiration, and moreover the frequent political changes in France during the 1880s and 1890s meant that continuity was hard to achieve. Further afield, the Americans and Japanese – both latecomers to the major league – were the only navies actually to carry out successful tactical fleet actions between 1866 and 1905 and, as will be seen in subsequent chapters, they kept it simple.

From the standpoint of the present day, the theory of naval power as it developed in the Ironclad Age had many limitations and showed considerable lack of foresight. By basing itself on the history of an exceptionally well-developed and mature form of warfare – the sailing-ship era – it sought to extract abiding principles, notably the achievement of sea command through decisive battle, but failed to show how such decisions might be reached given the entirely new technological tools becoming available and, worse, failed to predict the effect of the even more revolutionary technologies just round the corner.

It was particularly ironic that during the time the theories were being formulated, the main battle fleets of the powers were probably less capable of achieving decision by battle than they were either during the sailing-ship era or after about 1895. That is strongly suggested by the evidence set out in Chapter 1 of this book. It was just as well for the proponents of classical theory that between 1895 and 1905 several battles occurred that could be called truly decisive. These will of course be described in later chapters. What did well for the proponents of theory was perhaps less beneficial for the world as a whole, for the naval arms race was accelerated by this evidence that sea power really could work. The lessons of unrestricted submarine warfare, and of the inability of battle fleets to force a decision in modern conditions, were yet to come.

The French Navy was always eager to try out new theories, particularly any that might break the hold of British naval power, and their Squadron of Evolutions was the chief investigating instrument.

CHAPTER FOUR

THE AMERICAN CIVIL WAR

ABRAHAM LINCOLN, *President of the United States and Commander-in-Chief of the Union forces in the Civil War. Although bound up with the issue of slavery, the preservation or dissolution of the Union was the fundamental point of contention. The industrial power of the North, and its control of the sea perimeter, were governing strategic factors.*

THE AMERICAN CIVIL WAR

THE AMERICAN CIVIL WAR (1861–5) merits a chapter of this book to itself for several reasons. It was the first major war of the Ironclad Age proper; although the main characteristics of that age – armour, steam and shellfire – had all been employed in the Russian War of 1854–6, they had appeared piecemeal and their potential in synergy had gone largely unregarded. Under the impetus of war, both the American antagonists developed that potential quite rapidly. Secondly, and in consequence of that development, the war contained a great many 'firsts' and influenced thinking, worldwide, in many fields of maritime warfare. Finally, the spread of maritime operations, both in geography and in strategic and tactical scope, was unusually wide. In fact it can be argued that for sheer scale the Civil War, in the maritime arena no less than on land, was the most intense conflict of the whole period.

But from the point of view of those studying maritime warfare, and planning its instruments as best they could, the lessons appeared to be limited. The American Civil War was widely regarded as unique. Of course all wars are unique, but this was more unique than most. It had all kinds of problems and solutions that would be difficult to replicate elsewhere. Thus it would in many cases require a leap of imagination to draw the right lessons from the Civil War and apply them to European or Asian environments – a leap of which most analysts at the time proved incapable.

THE RIVAL STRATEGIES

The war began against a maritime backdrop. Fort Sumter was an outlier of the port of Charleston in South Carolina, the first state to secede from the Union after the election of President Abraham Lincoln in 1860. After the Confederacy had been formed by six other states joining South Carolina in February 1861, the garrison in Fort Sumter remained loyal to the Union. Relations became increasingly strained, and on 12 April the fort was attacked by Confederate forces and had to be evacuated. These were the first shots of a four-year struggle in which the objectives of the preservation or dissolution of the Union, and the abolition or continuation of slavery as an institution, were intertwined.

The Confederacy was subsequently joined by four more southern states, making eleven in all, though the degree of allegiance was variable. The Union mustered over twenty states, including five slave states which did not secede – and so again had some splits in their loyalties – and several vast tracts of as yet undeveloped territory in the West.

The sides were unevenly matched, most of all in industrial capacity. The Union had most of the apparatus of a modern state: coal, iron and water resources, extensive railway communications, manufacturing plant particularly for guns, munitions, armour plate and steam engines, and shipbuilding and repairing facilities. The South had far less of all of these, and in some areas, notably the production of rolled armour plate, hardly any. In manpower resources, too, the Northern states had a strong preponderance, particularly as the South was unable to tap any significant potential in its black population, who could naturally be expected to favour the Union with its promise of liberation.

Thus the South had to find a strategy that would neutralize its evident weaknesses and give a chance for secession to crystallize. It could not embark on a war of attrition, yet it needed to weary the North to the extent that the Union would no longer think it worth pursuing the struggle. There was one supplementary factor: if the Confederacy could persuade a European power to give substantial assistance, either as a belligerent or a friendly neutral, that could swing the balance both morally and materially and enable secession to become permanent. All these considerations meant that the South needed quick success both in the field and diplomatically, and the two would ideally work together to produce the desired result.

The Union strategy was in some elements articulate, in others confused. It recognized at once that the South had only one major economic asset, and that was its cotton production. This had habitually been exported not only to the North but to Europe. Therefore the first priority for the Union was to declare and enforce a blockade that would stop Southern export of cotton. This was duly declared by President Lincoln on 19 April 1861. The blockade continued with increasing effectiveness throughout the war, reinforced as will be seen by successive captures of Southern ports. The other priority was to disrupt the South's internal communications, which were in any case far from robust, and here waterborne forces would have a surprisingly large part to play. The often less articulated part of the Union strategy was underlying and simple: it was simply to exploit the North's superior staying power. Provided foreign intervention was avoided, this would ensure the war was won, and the Union preserved, eventually.

Geography, both by water and by land, played a critical part in the war. The conformation of coasts, rivers, plains and mountains was often peculiar and nearly always on a massive scale. In hindsight it was no wonder that the war lasted so long, though as is usual at the start of wars it was expected to be decided in a brief space of time.

One reason for this expectation was the relative proximity of the rival capitals. Washington for the Union, and Richmond for the Confederacy, were little more than 100 miles from each other, and Washington in particular regarded itself as vulnerable. Indeed, had Washington fallen, the quick success the Confederates sought would have been theirs and their standing in Europe, where sympathy for them was already apparent, enhanced. It was therefore fortunate for the North that the South's land forces, though spirited, were not well enough organized or supported to exploit their success at Bull Run in the summer of 1861.

The rival navies were scarcely better prepared. The Union, before secession, had a small navy of about forty steamers, none armoured and many deployed abroad, manned by 7,600 personnel. At the outbreak of war about one fifth of the 1,500 officers joined the Confederate navy, which managed to seize only a very few of the Union vessels in southern ports. A building race now began. The Union employed its own nascent warship-building resources; the Confederacy had perforce to adapt and improvise from its own very limited industry, and actively to seek purchases from Europe. In the line of commerce-raiders – of which more later – Confederate negotiators, led by James D. Bulloch, were moderately successful, but the procurement of major war vessels, though actively pursued, was almost entirely unrealized.

Meanwhile, with the limited resources available to it in 1861, the Union navy sought to enforce its declared blockade. This was only moderately effective, and in November of that year it did moreover nearly result in a serious breach of relations with Britain. The USS *San Jacinto* intercepted the British Royal Mail steamer *Trent* in the Old Bahama Channel and removed two envoys of the Confederacy alleged to be on their way to arrange blockade-running procedures with West Indian contacts. Feelings ran high on both sides of the Atlantic, the Royal Navy was redeployed, and plans were made in London for descents on the American coast while at the same time safeguarding the vulnerable border of

Seizure of two Confederate agents from the British mail steamer Trent *by the* USS San Jacinto *caused much resentment in Britain where public opinion at first tended to favour the Confederacy. The rift between Britain and the Union government took some time to heal.*

THE AMERICAN CIVIL WAR

Canada. It is argued by some modern historians that these moves were deterrent in nature; if so, it was a highly coercive form of deterrence. In any event, it worked. The envoys were given up, though Wilkes, the captain of the *San Jacinto*, remained a national hero in the USA and British public opinion took some years to shift away from hostility to the Union.

HAMPTON ROADS

It was not until 1862 that the sea war between North and South began in earnest. The focus was the sensitive area around the rival capitals; the position of the first battle was Hampton Roads, the sea inlet leading to Washington and Richmond. A Union blockading squadron was lying in the northern part of the Roads; it consisted of six wooden fully rigged vessels, the largest being of fifty guns.

It had been known to Union intelligence for some time that the Confederates were preparing to attack the blockading squadron, and for this purpose had refloated and adapted a vessel called the *Merrimac*, which they rechristened the *Virginia*. The *Virginia* was powered only by steam, clad in a double skin of armour totalling 4 inches thickness, and mounting twelve guns of between 6- and 9-inch calibre. She had in addition a ram and this was regarded as an important part of her armament.

On 8 March 1862 the *Virginia* made her way down the Elizabeth River and steamed across the Roads to attack the sloop *Cumberland*. Though her engine was badly underpowered, she succeeded in ramming and sinking the *Cumberland* while at the same time inflicting much damage and many casualties by shellfire on that ship and on the heavy frigate *Congress*, lying close by. Return fire from the Union ships had been ineffective; their round shot had simply bounced off the *Virginia*'s armour. Eventually, after spirited resistance, the *Congress* struck her flag. The remaining Union ships remained out of gunshot.

They did this partly to avoid being defeated one by one by this apparently invulnerable opponent, and partly because it was rumoured that substantial help was on the way. Indeed it came that night, in the shape of the Union ship *Monitor*. The *Monitor* was an even more radical vessel than the *Virginia*, for she was not an adaptation but a keel-up construction. The centrepiece of the ship was an Ericsson turret, mounting two 11-inch smooth-bore cannon firing solid shot. There was no other superstructure apart from a small armoured conning-tower and two tiny funnels. The rest of the craft was very low indeed in the water, her deck armour of 1-inch and side armour of 5-inch thickness extending the whole length and breadth of the ship. Her engine was more powerful and her steering more agile than those of the *Virginia* and she had one other advantage, a draught only about half that of the Confederate vessel.

But the *Monitor* had difficulty in the open sea, and her passage from New York had been hazardous even with the help of an accompanying tug and escorts. Nevertheless, when she anchored on the evening of 8 March in Hampton Roads, she brought great heart to the remaining Union ships.

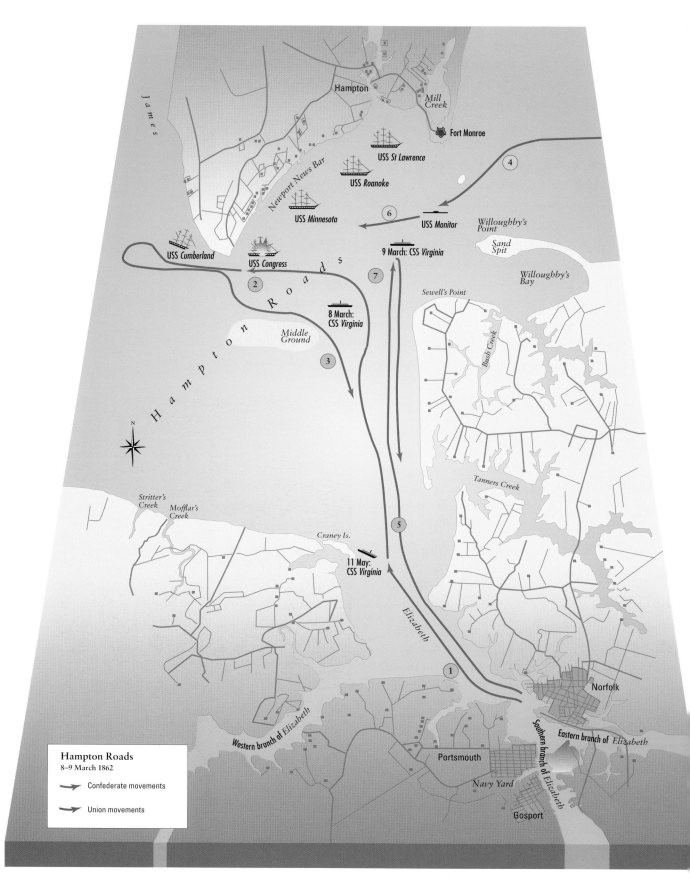

Hampton Roads
8–9 March 1862

→ Confederate movements

→ Union movements

The contest between the *Virginia* and the *Monitor* which took place on 9 March 1862 was recognized at the time, throughout the world, as epoch-making. It was the first fight between two ironclad vessels; as such it was later exhaustively discussed and analysed, and deductions – some right, some wrong and many a bit of both – drawn from it. It must, to watchers on the shore, have seemed strangely spasmodic, for the rate of fire of both vessels was extremely slow and the frantic efforts made to reload the guns and manoeuvre the ships into firing positions would not have been apparent.

Captain Buchanan of the *Virginia* had been wounded the previous day and command devolved on Lieutenant Catesby Jones, who at once sought to attack the USS *Minnesota*, still anchored in the northern part of the Roads, to repeat the success of the previous day. The *Monitor*, under the command of Lieutenant Worden, interposed herself and the battle began. It lasted some four hours, much of it at point-blank range, and included attempted rammings by both ships, the grounding of the *Virginia* in a further attempt to get at the *Minnesota*, and hauling off by the *Monitor* into shallow water in order to bring up ready-use ammunition. Eventually the *Virginia* retired up the Elizabeth River.

Both ships had sustained more than twenty hits and neither had suffered vital

Captain Franklin Buchanan of the CSS Virginia *and, later, the similar ironclad* Tennessee. *An officer of the United States Navy before the war, Buchanan resigned his commission to join the Confederate forces.*

8 March 1862: CSS *Virginia*, ex-Union steam frigate *Merrimac* hastily converted into an ironclad, sails from Norfolk Navy Yard to attack Union ships at anchor at the mouth of the James River

①

CSS *Virginia* opens fire on USS *Congress* while heading at full speed, about 6 knots, in order to ram USS *Cumberland*. *Virginia* withdraws, fires at the *Congress* and then rams the *Cumberland* for a second time, leaving her sinking and the *Congress* on fire

②

CSS *Virginia* returns to Norfolk Navy Yard

③

8 March, early evening: the ironclad turret ship USS *Monitor* arrives from New York

④

9 March: CSS *Virginia* appears at the mouth of the Elizabeth River apparently heading for USS *Minnesota*

⑤

USS *Monitor* steams to position herself to protect USS *Minnesota* which has run aground trying to move away from the approaching *Virginia*. *Monitor* opens fire on the *Virginia*

⑥

Hoping to get close to the *Monitor* the *Virginia* runs aground. After fifteen minutes of effort the *Virginia* moves free and gets close enough to fire a complete broadside at the *Monitor*, but with little effect. *Monitor* returns fire which also does little damage. After four hours of pounding each other the ships withdraw exhausted.

⑦

HAMPTON ROADS, 8–9 MARCH 1862

The first major sea action of the American Civil War, and the first action between armoured vessels, Hampton Roads is rightly considered a milestone in the Ironclad Age. The Confederate Ship Virginia, *created by side-armouring the ex-USS* Merrimac, *caused havoc amongst a conventional Union squadron until the arrival of the specially-constructed turret vessel USS* Monitor. *The ensuing four-hour action was tactically a draw, neither ship being able to inflict mortal damage on the other by gun or ram, but strategically it was a victory for the Union because it demonstrated that Confederate ironclad initiatives could be checked and that Union 'monitor' technology was sound.*

The success of the Monitor *in action led to series production of similar craft like the* Weehawken, *shown here. They were of great utility in river and coastal work, and in attacks on defended harbours. Their limited seakeeping ability was not critical in the circumstances of the war.*

damage. Moreover, there were no fatal casualties on either side; the most serious injury was to Lieutenant Worden, who behaved with heroism during the battle, though it might be said that his moral courage in making the difficult passage from New York was even more praiseworthy. One common feature of subsequent analysis was that the ammunition used by both sides was inappropriate; had the *Virginia* used solid shot, or the *Monitor* exploding shell, the result might have been different.

Tactically, it was a draw. Strategically, however, it was a great boost for the Union. The blockade was not broken, Washington was not threatened (there had been great apprehension of an assault supported by the *Virginia*), and most

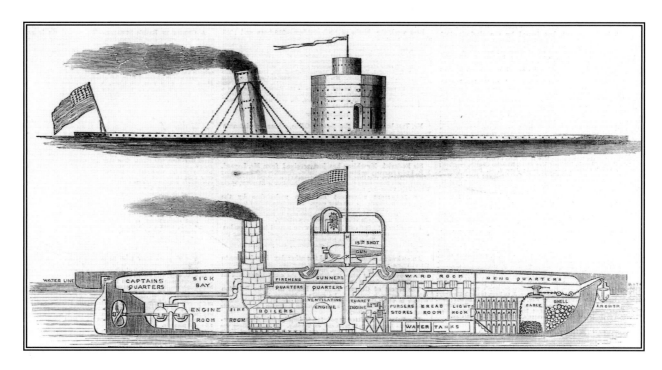

telling of all, the South had been denied a spectacular success – a success that might have made intervention on their side by one or more European powers more likely.

The *Monitor*'s showing confirmed in the eyes of the Union's naval administrators the utility of the monitor type, and by the end of the war well over forty of such craft had been constructed with further large numbers on the stocks. They ranged from relatively small river craft to twin-turret vessels, but it is fair to say that none were truly ocean-going and fighting in the open sea was not their forte.

THE MISSISSIPPI CAMPAIGN

An early major campaign undertaken by the Union navy, apart from the continuing blockade which occupied all sorts of craft, took place almost entirely in sheltered waters. This was the campaign for control of the Mississippi, a

*David Dixon Porter, the
Union Flag Officer in charge
of the northern jaw of the
pincer movement to achieve
control of the strategic
artery of the Mississippi.
Reserved and saturnine,
Porter was nevertheless an
exemplary exponent of
combined operations with
the land forces.*

strategic waterway if ever there was one, a means of lateral communication for whichever side held it and a barrier to the side that did not. It was of critical importance in the Civil War because it lay between the western states of the Confederacy, with their large agricultural production, and the eastern with their relatively large populations.

The campaign required good co-ordination between the land and waterborne forces of the Union, and on the whole got it, because the best of the Union commanders were involved: Grant in charge of the army and Porter and Farragut of the naval elements. The initial base was Cairo on the Illinois–Kentucky border, hundreds of miles from the sea. From here a thrust was launched up the Tennessee River to capture Fort Henry on 6 February 1862, with raids even further up the river to disrupt the fragile rail communications between east and west. In these operations and the capture of Fort Donelson on 13 February, gunboats with improvised armour were employed; though nothing like as invulnerable as later monitors, they gave some protection to crews and it was only when their vitals were penetrated that extensive casualties were sustained.

The scene was now set for a thrust down the Mississippi proper. This proceeded very rapidly, considering the distances involved and the primitive nature of many of the craft. A fort at Island No. 10 (long since swept away by changes in the great river's course) was captured on 8 April; Fort Pillow, another 70 miles downstream, on 5 June; and Memphis the next day. The river was now open as far as Vicksburg, a further 180 miles to the south: that would prove a harder nut to crack. There had been opposition on the water as well as from the forts; Confederate craft, many hastily adapted, appeared and attempted rammings were frequent. In all these operations the run of the river helped Porter's Union forces to get quickly past dangerous points and then engage from both upstream and downstream.

It was not so with the other jaw of the pincers, approaching up the Mississippi from its huge delta and seeking to pass New Orleans and link up with the forces approaching from the north. This force was commanded by Flag Officer Farragut (neither navy at this time recognized any rank higher than captain; Flag Officer was a temporary appointment). It contained no monitors, but had over twenty steam-powered vessels and mounted altogether over 150 guns.

In April 1862 Farragut crossed the Mississippi bar and approached the outer defences of New Orleans. These were at forts St Philip and Jackson, some 70 miles below the city. The river at that point is only a quarter of a mile wide, and the current strong. Apart from the forts, one on each bank of the river, the Confederates had assembled a boom consisting of hulks connected by a heavy chain; and there was a flotilla of small armed craft, mostly improvised, ready to oppose the assault.

After an initial bombardment conducted mainly by mortar-boats and lasting several days, and successful breaching of the boom by two gunboats, Farragut moved to pass the forts with his whole force, in a night operation. This, with a few minor hitches including the grounding for a time of the flagship, was successful; the forts were manned by inexperienced troops and resistance was not as tough as might have been expected. Once upstream Farragut was in a commanding position. He quickly disposed of the remaining Confederate force afloat, received the surrender of New Orleans on 25 April and that of the forts three days later. Once again the impact of this success was felt well beyond the North American continent. France still had considerable interest in Louisiana and had New Orleans held out for any length of time, internal pressure for her to intervene might have been hard to withstand.

Thus in mid 1862 there remained only Vicksburg between the Union and complete control of the Mississippi. But Vicksburg was a real obstacle. Farragut ran his force past it, in another night passage, on 28 June but rightly decided against any sort of waterborne assault. All he had proved, once again, was that

A typical action of the Mississippi campaign, near Vicksburg on 15 July 1862. The Confederate Arkansas *and Union* Carondelet *are in furious battle with frequent attempts to ram each other. Such actions were generally inconclusive but Union grip on the river steadily tightened.*

steamships given good organization and control could get past forts, but not necessarily reduce them. He was preoccupied too with three threats: the first was a Southern ironclad of some force, the *Arkansas*, which eluded destruction for some months; the second, much more serious, was fever among his crews; and the third, potentially catastrophic in view of the proximity of the Confederate armies, was the falling level of the river. Accordingly, Farragut withdrew his force to New Orleans. Porter remained above Vicksburg with the flotilla he had commanded with such distinction from the start of the campaign, far to the north.

The final clearance of the Mississippi did not take place until the spring of 1863. It was a classical combined operation. By then Grant had substantial land forces in position, and handled them with decision and daring. Meanwhile Farragut brought his force up river, attempting to pass much-reinforced Confederate works on the way. His success, using ships lashed together to protect the weaker of the pair, was only partial to begin with and incurred casualties which were heavy compared with those of the previous year. However, reinforced by some of Porter's command which had made their way past Vicksburg, he was

able to exert severe pressure on Confederate water communications. At the end of April Farragut turned over the command to Porter and rejoined his main force to the south, near Baton Rouge. Porter, meanwhile, co-operated with Grant in exemplary fashion, using his gunboats mainly for bombardment, and Vicksburg finally surrendered on 4 July.

CONFEDERATE COMMERCE RAIDING

Before turning to the third major element of the Union's waterborne campaigning – the blockade, supported by the progressive capture of Confederate ports – it will be right to deal with the only sea operations in which the Confederates can be said to have taken the offensive: commerce raiding.

It is doubtful if the South ever thought of this activity as a war-winner. The merchant marine of the Union was certainly extensive, and it was vulnerable, being very widely spread over the world's oceans. But the resources of the Confederate navy were not large, and at the start of the war they had few suitable ships to conduct an anti-commerce campaign. It is probably better to consider their objectives as mixed: partly to divert Northern effort away from the

General Ulysses S. Grant, chief architect of the Union clearance of the Mississippi. He showed an excellent grasp of the utility of waterborne forces throughout the campaign.

Captain Raphael Semmes of the Confederate commerce raider Alabama. *A chivalrous buccaneer, Semmes cruised the globe for two years, taking (and generally burning) over forty Union prizes and causing no loss of life. He was acquitted of all wrongdoing after the war.*

blockade, which was potentially extremely damaging to the South, and partly to sap Northern finances and business confidence. There was also a perceived public-relations bonus: by comparing Union harassment of neutral ships in the course of blockade with the sharply discriminate work, against the Union only, of the Southern cruisers, European powers would make comparisons favourable to the South, particularly if those cruisers acted with chivalry and humanity.

The *beau idéal* of the Confederate commerce-raider was undoubtedly Captain Raphael Semmes. He began in a small way in CSS *Sumter*, which sailed on her first cruise in June 1861. Her six-month career, during which she made eighteen captures of which eight were released, ended in Gibraltar in January

1862; three Northern ships lay in wait outside and Semmes sold the vessel. He was clearly in line for a more weighty command, and in August 1862 he got one: the *Alabama*, one of the most famous commerce-raiders of all time.

The *Alabama* began life as Hull No. 290 at Laird's Yard in Birkenhead. She had been ordered as a result of negotiations between Bulloch, Laird's and a go-between banking and shipping company, Fraser, Trenholm of Liverpool, England. She was a fast, fully rigged ship and in her Semmes had a worthy instrument. For nearly two years she ranged the oceans, coaling sometimes from captured vessels and sometimes from neutral ports. In that time Semmes made sixty-eight captures, nearly all of them sailing vessels, in seas as far off as the South Atlantic,

The fight between CSS Alabama *and USS* Kearsarge *off Cherbourg, 19 June 1864.* Alabama *had had two years' hard seagoing while* Kearsarge *was well supplied and prepared.* Alabama *sank after some hours' hot action.*

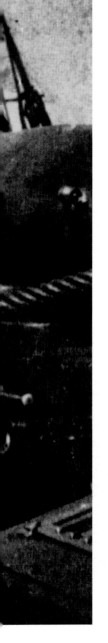

the Indian Ocean and the coasts of South East Asia. It is said that Semmes did not during that time take a single life. The crews of captured vessels were taken on board the *Alabama*, treated scrupulously well, and landed in populated places. When brought to trial after the war, Semmes was acquitted of any wrongdoing – by the victors.

The *Alabama*'s career nevertheless did not end in a glorious homecoming. She put in to Cherbourg, in some need of replenishment and repair, on 11 June 1864. News of her arrival was quickly telegraphed to Flushing where USS *Kearsarge* lay, and Captain Winslow at once sailed to intercept. The Union vessel, of approximately equal force to the *Alabama*, cruised off Cherbourg until 19 June when the *Alabama* came out to fight. The contest was watched by a vast crowd of spectators on the cliffs; someone said that half

Paris seemed to have come. The French ironclad *Couronne* escorted the *Alabama* to the edge of French territorial waters.

Semmes, though willing enough, may by then have had a tired crew and been tired himself. His ship had not been in action against serious opposition and indeed had fired few shots in anger in her two years. His ammunition was not in good condition after long exposure to the elements. He was thus at a disadvantage against an opponent who had had ample time to prepare and train and who, moreover, had been able to improvise some makeshift armour out of chain cable, while the *Alabama* had none. Thus, although both ships were manoeuvred with skill – it is said that they executed seven complete spirals in attempts to rake each other – the *Kearsarge* scored some vital hits on her adversary while suffering none herself. After two hours the *Alabama* struck her colours and less than an hour later sank by the stern. Most of the surviving crew were rescued, over sixty of them by the British yacht *Deerhound* which had been a spectator.

Several other Southern commerce-raiders made significant inroads on Northern shipping, though none achieved anything like the fame, or notoriety, of the *Alabama*. *Florida*, *Georgia* and *Shenandoah* all made numerous captures. Others, built or converted in Europe, never reached the Confederate navy, much less a cruising ground. Nevertheless, one count has placed the total number of

Above, a fast blockade-runner, a key component of Confederate strategy in moving cotton to the West Indies to finance the Southern war effort, and returning with military supplies. Beneath, a US monitor, whose limitations of speed and draught gave opportunities to blockade-runners, particularly those with local knowledge.

Union vessels captured during the war at 260, a considerable toll. It has been suggested by some authorities that 'the Union flag was driven from the seas'; that is too extreme a judgement, but there was undoubtedly a significant reduction – about 40 per cent – in the Union merchant fleet during the war, due more to re-flagging than to captures, but much of it no doubt caused by anxiety about commerce raiding.

What happened to the prizes? In previous wars, captured vessels had been sent in to port and thereafter adjudicated in the prize courts of the captor's country. In the nature of this war, the Confederates could have no such organization. In consequence, their general practice was to take from a prize anything of value to the cruise, put the crew in a place of safety and then burn the prize. It was a curious halfway-house between the old system of commerce warfare and the new, but it held none of the horrors of later unrestricted submarine campaigns.

The Union did not allow its naval forces to be dispersed on commerce protection missions, much less in convoy escort. Indeed in the circumstances of the time, with telegraphic networks only in their infancy and little administrative machinery overseas, the organization did not exist to enable the North to run an efficient protection system. The Union navy, therefore, went on with the blockade and the progressive reduction and capture of Southern ports.

THE UNION BLOCKADE: CHARLESTON, MOBILE, WILMINGTON

Up to the middle of 1863 the South could look with satisfaction on its arrangements to beat the blockade. The routes were mostly short runs to the West Indies, where the Bahamas became an entrepôt for Southern trade. Speed and stealth were of the essence, and specially designed or adapted blockade-runners provided both, particularly against the still thinly spread Union forces. The outward traffic in cotton and the inward traffic in arms and other essential military supplies were not unabated – there was massive unemployment in the cotton towns of Lancashire – yet they gave encouragement to the South that the war was sustainable.

But time was on the Union's side. Already by the middle of 1862 they had closed off the northern and southern ends of the Confederate Atlantic coastline: to the north, Hatteras and Roanoke Islands and the coastal towns of Norfolk and Beaufort had fallen to them, and to the south Port Royal near Savannah as well as several settlements in Florida were in their hands. On the Gulf of Mexico not only New Orleans, but the whole of the Mississippi delta, was under Union control. The possession of these places not only denied them to the Confederates, but gave the Union valuable advanced bases for further blockading and amphibious assault.

Nevertheless, three Southern ports continued to conduct a flourishing trade with the outside world, helped by daring blockade-runners, hydrographic conditions that helped to baffle the blockaders, powerful defensive works at their entrances, and – it was rumoured – connivance by some Northern entrepreneurs in extensive smuggling operations which, for example, ensured that a good deal of cotton leaving Southern ports made its way via Nassau to the industries of the North. These ports were Charleston and Wilmington on the Atlantic coast, and Mobile on the Gulf of Mexico.

The first objective among these three was Charleston. It had peculiar symbolic as well as practical value; it was after all where the war had started, and was regarded as a hotbed of secession. In January 1863 the task of capturing Charleston was entrusted to Rear Admiral (the rank had now become substantive) Du Pont, a Union officer who had previously distinguished himself in the capture of Port Royal. His force consisted mostly of wooden ships but he had one monitor, the *Montauk*, and the promise of more as they entered service. The Confederate defences were a series of forts, stoutly constructed and mounting some 250 guns in all; static mines, which had already proved themselves effective in the upper reaches of the Mississippi; and two newly constructed small ironclads, *Palmetto State* and *Chicora*, which initially operated with great spirit.

Subseqently the Union forces attempted to reduce the forts by bombardment from the monitors – of which there were eventually seven – but rates of fire were

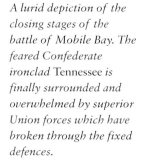

A lurid depiction of the closing stages of the battle of Mobile Bay. The feared Confederate ironclad Tennessee *is finally surrounded and overwhelmed by superior Union forces which have broken through the fixed defences.*

The least successful Union sea campaign of the war, the protracted assault on Charleston, lasted for several months of 1863, destroying the reputation of two Union Flag Officers and causing considerable losses to Union sea forces. Some Confederate forts were pounded to rubble but the complex as a whole held out.

very slow which, Du Pont complained, gave the defenders ample time to take cover before the next shot and then emerge to retaliate. A more determined effort was made on 7 April but return fire was heavy, and one monitor was sunk and another mined. Several similar efforts were made during the summer, but though Fort Sumter was battered to pieces and one other work abandoned, Charleston held out. The supersession of Du Pont by Rear Admiral Dahlgren made little difference.

A notable 'first' in this campaign was a series of attacks by Confederate vessels on the Union flagship, the *New Ironsides*, a broadside ironclad of conventional design. These employed spar torpedoes, the first fitted to a steam

The Union's New Ironsides *was probably the most sophisticated ship to emerge from the Civil War. She was unsuccessfully attacked by a Confederate submersible in 1863 and survived the conflict.*

Moored mines (often called torpedoes, as in Farragut's famous 'Damn the torpedoes! Full ahead!') were a weapon of choice for Confederate harbour defence. Their detonation however was uncertain, as at this time the Hertz Horn had not been invented.

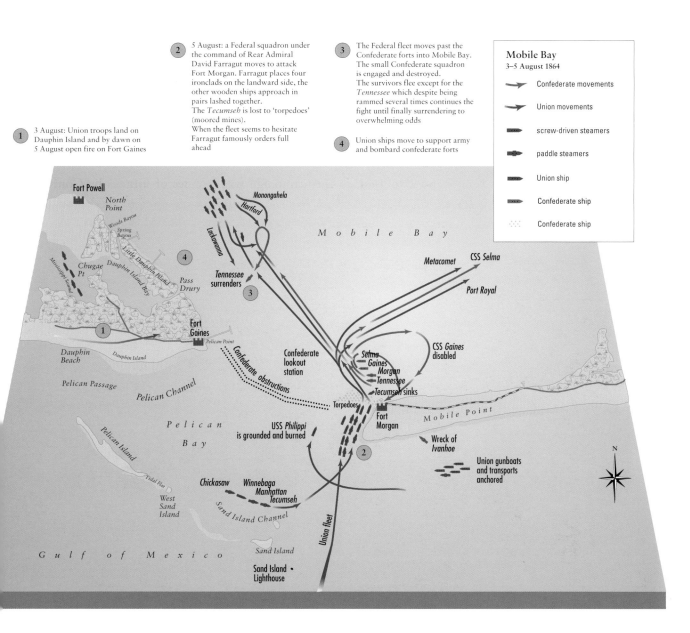

② 5 August: a Federal squadron under the command of Rear Admiral David Farragut moves to attack Fort Morgan. Farragut places four ironclads on the landward side, the other wooden ships approach in pairs lashed together.
The *Tecumseh* is lost to 'torpedoes' (moored mines).
When the fleet seems to hesitate Farragut famously orders full ahead

③ The Federal fleet moves past the Confederate forts into Mobile Bay. The small Confederate squadron is engaged and destroyed. The survivors flee except for the *Tennessee* which despite being rammed several times continues the fight until finally surrendering to overwhelming odds

① 3 August: Union troops land on Dauphin Island and by dawn on 5 August open fire on Fort Gaines

④ Union ships move to support army and bombard confederate forts

Mobile Bay
3–5 August 1864

→ Confederate movements

→ Union movements

screw-driven steamers

paddle steamers

Union ship

Confederate ship

Confederate ship

Fort Powell
North Point
Woods Bayou
Spring Bayou
Little Dauphin Island
Chugae Pt
Dauphin Island Bay
Mississippi Sound
Pass Drury
Dauphin Island
④
Lackawanna
Monongahela
Hartford
Tennessee surrenders
③
M o b i l e   B a y
Metacomet
CSS Selma
Port Royal
Confederate lookout station
CSS Gaines disabled
Selma
Gaines
Morgan
Tennessee
Tecumseh sinks
Fort Gaines
Pelican Point
Confederate obstructions
Torpedoes
Fort Morgan
M o b i l e   P o i n t
Dauphin Beach
Dauphin Island
Pelican Passage
Pelican Channel
P e l i c a n
B a y
USS *Philippi* is grounded and burned
②
Wreck of Ivanhoe
Union gunboats and transports anchored
Pelican Island
Tidal Flat
Chickasaw
Winnebaga
Manhattan
Tecumseh
Sand Island Channel
West Sand Island
Union fleet
N
G u l f   o f   M e x i c o
Sand Island
Sand Island Lighthouse

launch and the second to a semi-submersible called the *David*. Neither caused much damage, but they were portents of things to come. These duly came when in the next year a Confederate submarine, worked by a hand propeller, succeeded in sinking the Union vessel *Housatonic* with a spar torpedo. All hands in the submarine were lost. Even more portentous, in the eyes of some, was the successful attack by a steam launch under the command of Lieutenant Cushing of the Union, when in October 1864 the ironclad *Albemarle* was sunk, also by a spar torpedo.

Failure at Charleston caused the Union to consider next an attack on Mobile. This was just as tough a proposition as Charleston; the entrance was little more than a mile wide, half of this width being unnavigable shoal water, with strong forts on either side. The navigable channel was heavily mined; the only gap in the minefield, left for blockade-runners, was close under the guns of Fort

MOBILE BAY,
3–5 AUGUST 1864

In its assault on the strategically important Southern port of Mobile, Alabama, the US Naval force under Farragut faced every defence Confederate forces could muster. Ironclads led the approach followed by wooden ships lashed together. After the Tecumseh *was sunk by a mine the attackers pressed on and finally prevailed.*

A lurking menace in Union eyes, the ironclad Tennessee was probably the most powerful single unit produced by the Confederacy during the war. She carried two 110-pounder and four 95-pounder muzzle-loading rifled guns and was protected by 6-inch armour.

Morgan. A formidable ironclad, the *Tennessee*, built on *Virginia* lines but stronger and commanded by a recovered Captain Buchanan, lurked within the bay.

Farragut, placed in charge of this operation, was under no illusions. He waited until a force was gathered which he considered sufficient: four monitors and fourteen wooden vessels including his flagship, the *Hartford*. On 5 August 1864 they went in to the attack, the monitors leading, followed by the remaining ships in pairs lashed together. The leading monitor, the *Tecumseh*, anxious to engage the *Tennessee* which had already opened fire, attempted to cut across the minefield and was sunk with heavy loss of life. The Northern assault was in danger of breaking up in confusion.

It was at this point that Farragut made his celebrated decision to lead on, with his even more celebrated cry of 'Damn the torpedoes!'. The *Hartford* scraped over several mines – it was lucky for her that the Hertz Horn had not yet been invented – and the rest of the fleet followed. Once inside the bay, the action was by no means over; the *Tennessee* fought on for several hours until, surrounded by monitors which both bombarded and attempted to ram her, she surrendered. The forts held out for several days, and Mobile itself was not captured until 1865, though after August 1864 it was of course of no further use

Farragut was not only a highly effective commander, he fulfilled the need for heroes at this stage of the war. His courage and decisiveness in carrying on the assault on Mobile, after an early reverse when the Tecumseh *was sunk,* became the stuff of legend. The picture shows him at the shrouds of his flagship, USS Hartford.

General Benjamin Butler, a conspicuous failure in the initial unsuccessful assault on Fort Fisher, December 1864. Butler had much influence in Washington but his operational competence was highly questionable.

as a port of entry for Confederate blockade runners.

Charleston having proved itself obdurate, that left only Wilmington. This was protected at its Cape Fear entrance by Fort Fisher, which had been turned into a formidable work by the efforts largely of one man, Colonel Lamb of the Confederate forces. In fact the traffic of the blockade-runners up the Cape Fear River to Wilmington was still quite considerable even in 1864, because the conformation of the coast and depths over the bar made the stationing of blockading forces difficult. However, it was not until December of that year that a force was assembled to assault Fort Fisher.

The first attempt, with Rear Admiral Porter commanding the naval force and General Butler the land element, ended in failure. Butler was a man with much political influence but little

military competence, and he shied away from ordering an assault when a crack-brained scheme involving an explosion vessel, intended to detonate alongside the fort, fizzled out. Butler was replaced by the more determined General Terry, and on 15 January 1865 the fort was carried after the most ferocious bombardment of the war. Both navy and army personnel were employed in the assault and casualties among both were very heavy. This was the most truly 'joint' operation of all those on the coast, and though it was not without acrimony – Porter was not the easiest of colleagues – it was also the most successful. Wilmington was occupied on 22 February.

CONCLUSION

A few months later the war came to an end. Its maritime element had not always commanded the attention it deserved; both Presidents, Abraham Lincoln of the Union and Jefferson Davis of the Confederacy, tended to regard it as a sideshow compared with the shattering events on land. Probably that was an underestimate. The Northern blockade was certainly an essential element of strategy; had it been ineffective, the South could have held out much longer and, more importantly, maintained the sympathy of European nations much longer than it did. The clearing of the Mississippi was another essential part of the North's campaign and could not have been done without waterborne forces. Finally, the rolling up of the South's port and coastal resources must have had fatal effects on Southern morale and sealed their sense of isolation.

Tactical and material lessons abounded but, as was suggested at the start of this chapter, not all were correctly read. The spar torpedo and the ram were thought of as pointers to the future but turned out to be aberrations. Ironclads proved themselves, but the special conditions of coastal and riverine warfare led to a fashion for monitor-type configurations that were not suitable for other parts of the world. Submarine craft tweaked the imaginations of some. A lesson that was not learnt sufficiently was the importance of all-arms co-ordination in joint operations; there was even to the end of the war too much inter-service rivalry for effective employment of the forces available. But that, perhaps, was and is the hardest lesson of all in warfare.

The assault on Fort Fisher, at the mouth of the Cape Fear River leading to Wilmington, one of the blockade-runners' ports of entry to nearly the end of the war. Carried out on 15 January 1865, this was the most violent amphibious action of the conflict, with heavy casualties on both sides.

In the calm after the bloody assault on Fort Fisher, Union soldiers inspect a Confederate gun. The joint operation was conducted under the command of Admiral David D. Porter and General Alfred H. Terry.

CHAPTER FIVE

NAVIES AND IMPERIAL EXPANSION

*CONFIDENT YOUTH AT THE helm of Empire: Lieutenant
Roger Keyes and Able Seaman H. Brady on board HMS
Fame on return from operations against the Boxer Rising,
1900. A destroyer officer of the hell-for-leather school, Keyes
subsequently rose to the highest ranks of the Royal Navy.*

NAVIES AND IMPERIAL EXPANSION

Between 1815 and 1855, the European powers increased their stake in and influence on the rest of the world only gradually. Britain was consolidating the gains she had made in the eighteenth century, in India, Canada and Australasia. France in fact was more active in acquisition of territory, in Algeria and the Pacific islands. Russia was beginning a south-eastward expansion that was set to continue. The Netherlands maintained their East Indies possessions. Germany and Italy, of course, were not yet sovereign states through unification and had no conscious colonial ambitions. It was after 1855 that the most dynamic phase of imperial expansion began.

Britain had by that date acquired several strategic points that, as it turned out, were to serve as springboards: Singapore in 1819, Malacca in 1824, Natal in 1843. Sea power, in its broadest sense, had been both a driver and a facilitator in these acquisitions, and it was sea power both civil and military that became a dominant factor in the next half-century's rapid imperial development. That power was wielded not only by Britain but to an extent by all the colonial nations.

The technology of the Ironclad Age was an immense multiplier of European influence and control. Steam was its greatest asset. As will become apparent in this chapter, the ability of naval steam-driven ships and craft to penetrate to seats of indigenous power was critical to many colonial enterprises. On the civil side, the mobility and flexibility of steam-driven merchant ships enabled an unprecedented surge of trade. It was said that trade followed the flag; it was just as true, if not so sonorous, to say that the flag followed trade. In this field, again, Britain was predominant. The British merchant fleet was four times as large as any other.

THE INDIAN MUTINY: 1857–8

Large sections of the Indian Army, in the employment of the Honourable East India Company, mutinied in the spring of 1857 and the whole British position in India was threatened. While British regiments in the subcontinent did their best to contain the mutineers, they were outnumbered and all possible reinforcement was required. Three Royal Naval ships at Hong Kong, which previously had been positioned on the west coast of South America, were detached and arrived at Calcutta in August. One, the *Sanspareil*, landed a substantial party to garrison the main fort of Calcutta but then returned to the Far East. The other two, the frigates *Shannon* and *Pearl*, remained in Indian waters and contributed greatly to the suppression of the mutiny.

They did so in a manner that became a pattern for the colonial operations of the next half-century. The ships themselves were of too deep a draught to go far up river, so a large proportion of each ship's company was disembarked either to shore or to rafts that were then towed up by commandeered steam-driven craft, taking with them not only small arms but as many of the larger guns as could conveniently be landed. The naval brigade so formed, often including a high proportion of Royal Marines, generally had both artillery and infantry roles.

The *Shannon*'s brigade, over 500 strong, took two months to cover the 700 miles from the mouth of the Ganges to Allahabad where in the second half of October 1857 they disembarked and took part in a series of actions before Kanpur and Lucknow. Co-operation between army and naval units was excellent, and continued so for the first three months of 1858 as the British steadily gained the upper hand. The brigade's return to their ship was marred by the death from wounds, aggravated by smallpox, of their outstanding commanding officer, Captain William Peel.

The *Pearl*'s brigade under Captain Sotheby was about 200 strong and took a more northerly route in the steamer *Jumna*, operating with a mixed Field Force, including a high proportion of Gurkhas, under the overall command of Colonel Rowcroft. They fought a series of actions along and to the north of the Ghogra River throughout 1858 and took part in the last major action of the war at Tulsipur near the Nepalese border. Once more the adaptability of the naval contingent and their ability to handle heavy weapons in a variety of situations were of great help to the force and earned high praise from the army authorities.

THE FAR EAST: 1856–65

The Opium War of 1840–41 had not only consolidated the British position in Hong Kong but secured important concessions in Canton from which European and United States' trade with China could continue to expand. However, instability within China gave opportunities in the late 1850s for local initiatives, from piracy to governmental measures, that interfered with Western interests and were thought to threaten the whole basis of trade.

In consequence the British Commander-in-Chief, Rear Admiral Sir Michael Seymour, directed an attack on the defences of Canton. The outlying forts were taken in October 1856, and the fleet commanded the approaches to Canton. Further progress was bogged down by unexpectedly strong Chinese resistance on the ground and the skilful diplomacy of Commissioner Yeh, and a stalemate persisted throughout 1857, the British effort being weakened by the need to divert forces to India in consequence of the mutiny. The only significant British success that summer was in Fatshan Creek, above Canton, where a large force of Chinese war junks was routed and burnt; steam, firepower and discipline were the keys to success.

In December a French squadron arrived to reinforce the British off Canton, and troops from both countries became available. The main assault (including a British naval brigade of 1,500 men) went in, after an ultimatum, on 28 December 1857 and the city was effectively occupied by 30 December. It was one thing, however, to make a military conquest of a city of a million people, and quite

OPPOSITE: *An over-confident and casual Commander-in-Chief, Admiral Sir James Hope (far right – note the muddy shoes!) suffered the only major British naval defeat of the Ironclad Age at the mouth of the Peiho, 1858.*

The Battle of Fatshan Creek, 1 June 1857. In this inlet above Canton a large body of Chinese war junks was defeated by British forces under Admiral Seymour and Commodore Henry Keppel.

another to administer it. The Chinese authorities knew this very well, and the situation entered a new sort of stalemate.

Negotiation with the Imperial Chinese Government was considered necessary. But a proposed meeting in Shanghai failed to materialize, and the Western plenipotentiaries thought it necessary to negotiate from a position of strength. Naval forces were therefore sent north, and an ultimatum delivered to the commander of the Taku forts, at the mouth of the Peiho and commanding the approaches to Tientsin and Peking. On expiry of the ultimatum, combined British and French forces were landed under cover of fire from some eleven warships. Resistance was overcome without much difficulty and the fleet moved through to Tientsin, where the Chinese authorities signed a treaty on 27 June 1858. The USA and Russia were also parties. The treaty gave many concessions, commercial and diplomatic, to Western powers.

Difficulties soon arose over interpretation of the treaty, and almost exactly a year later a new team of British and French envoys was charged with ensuring Chinese compliance. Once more it was deemed necessary to pass the Taku forts and take a naval force through to Tientsin. In the interval, however, the Chinese had much improved the fortifications. The British under their new Commander-in-Chief Sir James Hope were over-confident, the French forces were mostly elsewhere, and the American presence was nominally neutral. An assault by naval landing parties alone was frustrated by boom defences and fixed obstructions, heavy fire from the forts, and most of all by mud, which made the approach to the forts almost impassable. The British were repulsed with heavy loss. Some *de*

facto non-firing help was given by the US force under the direction of Commodore Tattnall USN, who remarked famously that 'blood is thicker than water'.

It was in the spirit of the times that this reverse should be regarded as an 'insult' to be avenged. But not until the next year was sufficient force assembled to make sure of a successful attack on the Taku forts. The British and French troops which landed at Pehtang in August 1860 amounted to over 20,000, and in the face of this overland attack, supported by fire from the gunboats, the Taku forts surrendered on 21 August. The army units went on to Tientsin and subsequently to Peking, where a further treaty, more favourable to Western interests than that of Tientsin, was signed on 24 October.

The situation in China was confused by the Taiping rebellion against central government, which had been going on since 1858. The years from 1860 to 1862 saw British policy endeavouring to protect the Western interest on the Yangtse and particularly at Shanghai, already a most important

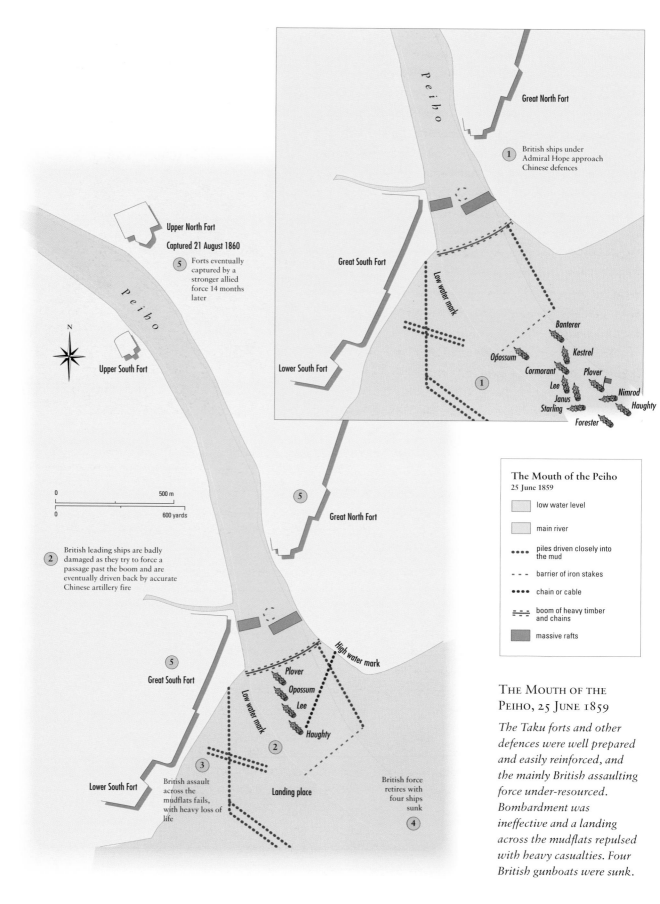

Great North Fort

British ships under
Admiral Hope approach
Chinese defences ①

Great South Fort

Low water mark

Lower South Fort

Banterer

Kestrel

Opossum

Cormorant

Plover

Lee

Nimrod

Janus

Haughty

Starling

Forester

①

Upper North Fort

Captured 21 August 1860

Forts eventually
captured by a
stronger allied
force 14 months
later ⑤

Upper South Fort

P e i h o

N

⑤

Great North Fort

British leading ships are badly
damaged as they try to force a
passage past the boom and are
eventually driven back by accurate
Chinese artillery fire ②

⑤

Great South Fort

High water mark

Plover

Opossum

Low water mark

Lee

Haughty

②

③

Landing place

Lower South Fort

British assault
across the
mudflats fails,
with heavy loss of
life

British force
retires with
four ships
sunk

④

0	500 m
0	600 yards

The Mouth of the Peiho
25 June 1859

	low water level
	main river
••••	piles driven closely into the mud
- - -	barrier of iron stakes
●●●●	chain or cable
═══	boom of heavy timber and chains
▬	massive rafts

THE MOUTH OF THE PEIHO, 25 JUNE 1859

*The Taku forts and other
defences were well prepared
and easily reinforced, and
the mainly British assaulting
force under-resourced.
Bombardment was
ineffective and a landing
across the mudflats repulsed
with heavy casualties. Four
British gunboats were sunk.*

trading port on the China coast. Commanding officers of gunboats, often only of lieutenant's rank, found themselves in acutely difficult diplomatic situations trying to support a policy that was overtly non-interventionist but often, effectively, favoured the central government.

Rear Admiral Kuper, who succeeded Hope in February 1862, successfully tapered off British operations against the Taipings. He had other preoccupations, further afield in Japan. That country too was in confusion, brought on partly by the decay of the Shogunate and partly by efforts from the Western powers, in the wake of Commodore Perry's visit in 1853, to open up Japan to trade – a deeply divisive issue. Isolated attacks were made on Western nationals and consulates in the autumn of 1862 and these were taken extremely seriously by the British, who demanded reparation.

Influential forces in Japan remained split and by mid 1863 the faction demanding the removal of all foreigners appeared to be getting the upper hand. French, Dutch and American ships were fired on in the Strait of Shimonoseki and retaliated with a bombardment and landing. In August Kuper was instructed to take coercive action against the Satsuma clan, which led the anti-foreigner party. Between 15 and 17 August seven of his ships carried out a bombardment of Kagoshima in the southern island of Kyushu. All were wooden-hulled but steam-powered, and as was mentioned in Chapter 1, their breech-loading guns did not perform well. In spite of this the damage to Kagoshima was considerable and the effect on Japanese opinion immense; for reasons of expediency, the majority of the ruling elements now favoured opening the country to foreign trade and influence.

One Japanese faction however remained opposed, and gained control over the Strait of Shimonoseki which lay at the western entrance to the Inland Sea. In the summer of 1864 Kuper sailed from Yokohama and joined up with French, Dutch and American forces to force the Strait. Altogether eighteen vessels were assembled, mounting nearly 300 guns in all; a British screw line-of-battle ship, the *Conqueror*, was the largest present, and it was probably the last time such a British ship was in action.

The operation was a sequential one from east to west, softening up each set of forts in turn by bombardment and following up with landings by detachments from all the nations involved, to spike guns that could not be moved and bring off those that could. It lasted three days, from 5 to 8 September, and was completely successful in military terms, with light casualties on the attackers' side. It was also successful in its immediate political effects; the Strait was opened and treaties satisfactory to the West were concluded with Japan.

Vice Admiral Augustus Kuper, British Commander-in-Chief on the China Station, 1862–4. His firmness and diplomacy were fully tested by the Taiping rebellion in China and difficulties with Japan.

*Sailors from four countries –
France, the Netherlands, UK
and USA – join to inspect
and spike Japanese guns on
the shore of the Strait of
Shimonoseki after
bombardment and landing
by the combined fleets,
5–8 September 1863.*

THE NEW ZEALAND WAR: 1860–64

The conflict in the North Island of New Zealand, in which Maori forces under the leadership of William King sought to check or reverse the acquisition of land by settlers, was conducted mainly by units of the British army, but naval forces and auxiliaries provided essential mobility in a largely coastal campaign. Land communications were unsuitable for the movement of large bodies of troops, and intelligence as to the next upsurge of opposition was difficult to come by until it had occurred, so that reaction by sea was the most likely, and usually the only possible, pattern of operations.

Naval brigades, sometimes numbering some hundreds, were frequently landed to co-operate with the army and distinguished themselves in several hot actions, some of which involved heavy casualties against the stiff opposition of the Maoris, generally operating from wooden stockades. British tactics were often unimaginative, relying too much on frontal assault, not the best way of conducting what turned out to be a war of attrition. Eventually superior numbers and *matériel* prevailed, but it was to the credit of both sides that relations were not permanently undermined.

An anti-'piracy' operation. During a Peruvian uprising in 1877 the turret-ship Huascar *joined the rebels and was alleged to have committed piratical acts. She was engaged by the British cruiser* Shah, *with one consort, and though the action was inconclusive she surrendered to government forces next day.*

THE SECOND ASHANTI WAR: 1873–4

British interest in the Gold Coast of West Africa (now Ghana) was in 1870 confined to a few small enclaves under British protection, established originally as bases for operations against the slave trade and latterly as outlets for the trade in palm oil. The coast was inhabited by the Fanti tribe, who looked for protection from the British fort at Cape Coast Castle. Up the Prah River, about 100 miles inland, was the country of the Ashanti, a warlike tribe with a well-organized and far from ill-equipped army.

A quarrel arose with King Kofi of the Ashanti. The British had acquired a further fort at El Mina from the Dutch and refused to pay any further subvention. Kofi's army, estimated at 30,000 men, invested the coast country and in April 1873 defeated Fanti tribal levies. British forces on station were extremely thin. There were five warships, none larger than a paddle corvette, and 110 Royal Marines. On 7 June the paddle corvette *Barracouta* arrived to supplement the force, and her captain, Edmund Fremantle, took charge of operations.

An initial success by landing parties of Marines and the *Barracouta*'s seamen at El Mina checked the Ashanti and in July reinforcements arrived in the form of

the *Rattlesnake*, with a West Indian Regiment and Commodore John Commerell, closely followed by the *Simoon* troopship with 200 more Royal Marines. Commerell decided on an expedition up the Prah River and this ended in near-disaster when the boats, in tow of a steam launch, were ambushed from the bank. Commerell and several others were wounded, but the launch was unscathed and managed to extract the expedition. A further reverse at the village of Chamah left several dead, and the village was bombarded and burnt in retribution. This was a pattern that was to be repeated on many occasions in this and other wars.

Further bombardments of coastal villages were followed by a blockade of the coast, designed to stop arms supplies reaching the Ashanti. In London it was

(1) 1873: Ashanti raids overwhelm small British garrisons on coast

(2) June 1873: seven Royal Navy ships on patrol station off the Gold Coast

(3) August 1873: Chamah attacks naval boat party. Retaliatory naval raid burns Chamah

(4) October–November 1873: British forces under Major General Sir Garnet Wolseley, including a naval brigade of about 350, march north

(5) January–February 1874: British force advances on Kumasi, the Ashanti capital, which is captured and razed. The British then withdraw to the coast

THE ASHANTI CAMPAIGN, 1873–4

A typical campaign of imperial expansion, the Ashanti operations began as a purely naval affair with small-scale expeditions in support of British interests. After escalation leading to *full-scale war against the Ashanti in the interior, the British Army under Sir Garnet Wolseley played the principal role but a naval brigade formed part of the force. After the* *major battle of Amoaful and occupation of Kumasi the British force withdrew in good order to the coast, 'pacification' having in Wolseley's view been achieved.*

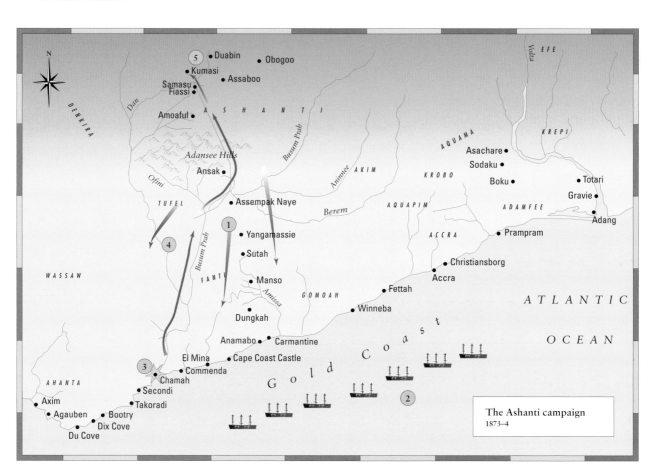

The Ashanti campaign 1873–4

doubted whether these measures would have the desired effect of causing Kofi to withdraw his forces, and the Cabinet was persuaded by Major General Sir Garnet Wolseley to mount a full-scale expedition against Kumasi, the Ashanti capital. After meticulous preparation three regiments reached the Gold Coast in early October 1873.

Wolseley's campaign belongs to military history, since after the unopposed landings waterborne forces had little part except to keep the coastal bases secure. The Prah River was an obstacle rather than a strategic waterway. Nevertheless, Wolseley made use of a naval brigade of 250 bluejackets and 100 Royal Marines, and they gave distinguished service, sometimes as rear and sometimes as advanced guard, to Kumasi and back. There were many skirmishes and one major battle, at Amoaful, in which stiff Ashanti resistance was overcome. The expedition was fêted in London on its return in April 1874.

The Ashanti War demonstrated that while sea power on its own could control a littoral, it was unlikely to have decisive influence on a wide hinterland, particularly if this was the seat of a well-organized and populous state. If such a state was hostile, troops on the ground were required to resolve the situation. The navy recognized this, and willingly provided brigades to fight far inland if need be; a further and more extreme example occurred in the Zulu War of 1878–9, when after the débâcle of Isandhlwana a brigade nearly a thousand strong was put together to fight alongside the army, miles from the sea, and quickly learned to form square with military precision.

A convoy of British sick and wounded returning to the coast from the inland expedition to Kumasi during the Ashanti War, 1873–4.

THE SUDAN CAMPAIGN: 1884–5

While the bombardment of Alexandria in 1882 (see Chapter 6) had greatly weakened Arabi Pasha's influence and secured Alexandria as a port of entry, Egypt remained rudderless and the Sudan, which had been under Egyptian suzerainty since 1822, was in revolt. The Dervish insurgents were led by the self-proclaimed Mahdi. The British Government under Gladstone was reluctant to become involved but, nevertheless, pressed for General Gordon to be appointed to Khartoum to supervise Egyptian withdrawal from Sudan. He departed for Khartoum in January 1884.

For many months the British government recognized no threat to Gordon or his mission. However, in the eastern Sudan they saw need for military action. The Dervishes in that area had defeated two Egyptian forces under British officers (Hicks Pasha in October 1883 and Baker Pasha in February 1884). Dervish control of the western shore of the Red Sea would, it was thought, pose a threat to sea communications with India – a prime tenet of British policy. In consequence, a British force of five infantry and two cavalry regiments from Egypt, supported by a naval brigade of 550 and six Gardiner guns, was landed in the eastern Sudan. All forces were ashore by 28 February 1884. In a series of hard-fought and sometimes touch-and-go actions over the next two weeks this force

Charles G. Gordon (left) and William Gladstone. A semi-legendary figure, 'Chinese Gordon' was dispatched in January 1884 to attempt negotiations with the regime in the Sudan. His idiosyncratic approach, combined with the reluctance of the Gladstone government to react to the danger in which he was placed, led to the belated Sudan campaign of 1884–5 and his death in Khartoum in January 1885.

under Major General Graham broke for the time being the power of Osman Digna's Hadendoa tribesmen, possibly up to 10,000 in number, who were allied to the Mahdi. This was an operation strictly limited in aim and scope, and the troops were ordered back to Egypt.

Throughout the summer, communications between Gordon and British representatives in Cairo became more and more difficult; the telegraph from Khartoum had been cut in March. There were strong indications that Gordon was behaving erratically and exceeding his brief. Gladstone continued to refuse to countenance full-scale intervention in the Sudan. In fact it was not until 19 September that Wolseley was instructed to mount a relief expedition.

This was to use the Nile as the main approach route. There were other options, including an advance from the Red Sea coast (which Graham would have been ideally poised to mount in March, although the terrain was difficult) and a short cut across a great bend in the river, but Wolseley was a man of strong opinions and had his way. The navy's part in the subsequent campaign was confined to a series of stations along the Nile to help and advise vessels passing the cataracts, and the formation of a small brigade of Royal Marines and bluejackets to supplement the newly formed camel corps and to provide and man, critically as it turned out, a couple of Gardiner guns. The brigade, like all naval operations in the campaign, was under the command of Lord Charles Beresford. Still a Commander, he was already 'Charlie B.' to the whole fleet.

Sailors on camels were an unaccustomed sight, but in the actions at Abu Klea in early January 1885 and the subsequent short-cut march across the great bend

Commander Lord Charles Beresford in the commandeered river steamer Safieh *goes up the Nile to rescue Gordon's would-be rescuer, Colonel Sir Charles Wilson, in February 1885. The jingoism of the occasion was offset by a display of genuine courage and resourcefulness.*

in the Nile – a change of plan by Wolseley – they and the Gardiner guns did well and by 21 January were before Metemmeh, only 80 miles short of Khartoum. The naval artificers were now called on to adapt and arm two river steamers for the final passage. Beresford, suffering from boils in an unfortunate place, was forced to remain in reserve and it was Colonel Sir Charles Wilson in the lead steamer who finally came in sight of Khartoum on 28 January, to find that the residency had fallen and Gordon was dead. His return, under fire and suffering grounding and breakdowns, was saved from disaster by the remaining steamer, the *Safieh*, commanded by a Beresford sufficiently recovered to control operations from a bed specially made up on the upper deck. In the week from 29 January to 4 February the *Safieh* ran every conceivable hazard, including shell damage to the engine which was repaired with hardihood amounting to heroism by Chief Engineer Benbow and his artificers. She returned, with Colonel Wilson and his party, to Gubat, north of Metemmeh.

The main British campaign on the Nile was over, and could indeed be said to have failed in its purpose. However, it was judged necessary to salvage some prestige for British arms, and the opportunity was presented by the resurgence of Osman Digna and the Hadendoa forces in the Eastern Sudan. A force under General Graham, similar to but somewhat larger than that of 1884, was formed and as was now usual a naval brigade formed part of it. The subsequent battle of Tofrek ('McNeill's zareba') on 22 March 1885 followed, as its subtitle suggests, a familiar pattern of headlong assault by Dervishes on a fortified British square, and resulted in very heavy casualties on the part of the Hadendoa, whose power diminished greatly from then on.

The Sudan campaigns had many of the elements of Greek tragedy: hubris and nemesis were in abundance, with strong contributions from misunderstanding and indecision. One of the ironies was that approval was given in January 1885 for a railway to be constructed between Suakin, on the Red Sea coast, and Berber on the Nile. Had this been given eleven months before, the situation would have been entirely different. The laborious advance up the Nile, which gave such limited opportunities for the exploitation of sea power, would not have been needed. But, of course, at that time the government in London had recognized no further need to intervene.

THE FRENCH NAVY AND IMPERIAL EXPANSION

Before 1880, France's expansion beyond the shores of the Mediterranean had been limited to extending control in Senegal – an up-river expedition not unlike the British–Ashanti War, though in this case conducted against a Muslim *jihad* – and co-operation with other Western powers on the coasts of China and Japan.

In the 1880s and 90s, however, a marked upsurge of French activity took place. Assessing that the Berlin Congress of 1878 had given them a free hand in Tunisia, French forces occupied strategic points in that country, particularly Bizerte which turned out to be an excellent potential base. From here and from

neighbouring Algeria, already in French hands, French forces in the next twenty years spread southwards across west Africa to meet forces inserted by sea in Guinea, the Ivory Coast, Dahomey and Congo. This inevitably brought them into confrontation with the British who were doing much the same thing in Nigeria, Gambia and the Gold Coast, and matters finally came to a head far to the eastward at Fashoda on the Upper Nile in 1898.

It was in this situation that battle-fleet supremacy took a hand. Mobilization quickly convinced the French that they could not match the British fleet and that their forces abroad would inevitably become isolated. They also feared for the security of their bases; it was known that British plans for assaults, not only *outre-mer* but on metropolitan France, existed. The situation was resolved in Britain's favour.

Meanwhile, in the Indian Ocean, France had spread her influence in the great island of Madagascar, where an important base was acquired at Diego Suarez. In the Far East she was even more active. A full-scale war against China began with a major naval battle off Foochow in August 1884, and France in consequence gained control of Indo-China with its rich rice-growing areas. At the same time

Admiral Courbet and his staff on the bridge of his flagship. Courbet was the principal commander in all the initiatives of the French Navy in the Far East in the mid 1880s. French influence from the Gulf of Thailand to Taiwan was strong and France acquired rich possessions in the area.

A Chinese view of the
repulse of French forces at
Keelung, Formosa (Taiwan)
in 1884. The picture needs to
be studied in detail to gather
its full impact.

the French Navy established a semi-permanent base at Keelung, in Taiwan, and the notion of exploiting the considerable coal reserves of that island was current.

It is worth noting that a great part of this activity took place under naval auspices. The French colonial administration was the responsibility of the Ministry of Marine until 1893. Jules Ferry, the Minister for much of the period, took personal control of policy and sometimes even of operations, and the Naval Infantry and Artillery were heavily involved in colonial work. The central figure in the Indo-China conflict was Admiral Courbet. The *Jeune École* were wholeheartedly in favour of colonial expansion, which they saw as an out growth of the indirect approach to maritime strategy that they advocated. Admiral Aube, in particular, regarded a chain of bases running through Bizerte, Obock (Djibouti), Diego Suarez and Tonkin to Keelung as having the potential for cutting British sea communications in the event of war.

Jules Ferry, a highly influential French statesman of the 1870s and 1880s. As Minister of Marine during much of the period, he was also responsible for colonial administration and expansion.

THE BOER WARS: 1880–81 AND 1899–1902

The First Boer War resulted from British annexation of the Transvaal (with the acquiescence of some Boer leaders) in 1877 and subsequent failure to give sufficient autonomy to the settlers. The small and scattered British garrison forces, led by General Colley, were supplemented by a naval brigade that in the end amounted to some 200 men with two Gatling guns and three rocket tubes, provided by ships on the South Africa Station.

The war was characterized by a series of command failures, the worst being at Laing's Nek and Majuba Hill. The latter, in which a British force of several hundred, commanded with well-nigh unbelievable complacency by Colley personally, was routed with more than 50 per cent casualties, and cost the naval brigade thirty-six men killed. The war ended with a provisional peace treaty which Kruger, the Transvaal leader, hoped had secured its independence.

The Second Boer War had many roots – economic, cultural and political – and analysis will be for other books in this series. It is enough to say that when war broke out in October 1899, the Boer forces in the Transvaal and Orange Free State, armed with modern weapons, outnumbered the British garrisons in Natal and Cape Province by about four to one, and their advance was regarded as a threat to the whole British position in southern Africa.

The most urgent requirement to stiffen British forces was guns with a reasonable throw-weight. The navy was the only immediate source of reinforcement. Fortunately for Britain the large, fast cruisers *Powerful* and *Terrible* were in the area, and were diverted to Simonstown to supplement the small Cape Squadron consisting of the *Doris* and *Monarch*. Moreover, the *Terrible* was commanded by Captain Percy Scott, the navy's greatest gunnery expert and a man of highly inventive mind.

British by 1895

Boer Republic

German territory

Portuguese territory

→ naval brigade

→ Jameson raid 1895

→ British advance

→ major Boer raids 1899–1901

① 14 October 1899: naval brigade (360) leaves Simonstown

② HMS *Powerful* to Durban with adapted naval guns

③ Late October 1899: HMS *Powerful* guns to Ladysmith by rail

④ November 1899 – February 1900: naval brigade (450) with two 4.7-inch guns, plus six 12-pounders support Buller's advance to relieve Ladysmith

⑤ From 29 October 1899: naval guns with besieged force (Captain Lambton)

⑥ October 1899 – February 1900: naval brigade with four 12-pounder guns supports Methuen's advance on Kimberley (Captain Prothero)

⑦ March 1900: naval brigade continues to support Roberts to Bloemfontein (Captain Bearcroft) and on towards Johannesburg and Pretoria in June 1900

⑧ May–August 1900: 'Grant's Guns', separate four-month campaign against de Wet (Commander Grant)

The first guns to land were 12-pounder field guns on mountings designed by Scott. But he quickly showed he could do better. Spurred by desperate messages from Sir George White in Ladysmith, requesting heavier metal, he devised transportable mountings for two 4.7-inch guns and sent them round by sea to Durban in *Powerful*. They went up to Ladysmith by train, and were followed by an even more ambitious project, a 6-inch piece prepared within four days from the time it was disembarked.

In the subsequent siege of Ladysmith, the naval brigade commanded by Captain Hedworth Lambton probably made the difference between holding out and surrender. Numbering about 280 all told, out of a total besieged force of some 12,000, it was small in terms of manpower but its firepower was critical. With two 4.7-inch and four 12-pounders, it provided the majority of artillery

NAVAL BRIGADES IN THE
SECOND BOER WAR

The Royal Navy's critical contribution was the provision of firepower at the outset of operations: 4.7-inch and 12-pounder guns were disembarked from ships and, with their crews, joined the campaigns in Natal and the Orange Free State as well as the siege of Ladysmith.

support to oppose a Boer field train totalling twenty-two guns of similar calibre. Strict economy of ammunition had to be exercised, as did economy of everything else; horse was on the menu from Day 76 of the siege.

A determined attack by the Boers on 6 January 1900 was repulsed after an all-day fight and a costly counter-attack to clear the last of the Boers from the field. That day's action was notable for the conduct of a naval Gunner, Mr Sims, who directed the fire of the guns, deployed his crews as infantry when circumstances dictated, and led a bayonet charge. He was directly promoted to Lieutenant. Ladysmith was not relieved for another seven weeks. By that time the naval brigade had lost six men killed, but another twenty-seven had died of disease: a not unusual proportion for this war.

The second naval brigade was again based upon disembarked guns and consisted of some 450 men with two 4.7-inch on wheels and six 12-pounders. Under the command of Captain Jones of the *Forte* they joined General Buller's column moving up from Durban to the relief of Ladysmith. On 15 December 1899, at the battle of Colenso, the naval 12-pounder guns were lucky (or prudent) enough not to be deployed as far forward as the fire-eating Colonel Long had put his 15-pounder pieces; the latter were blanketed with rifle fire while the naval guns were recovered, though with difficulty. But Colenso was a bad reverse. It was only after two more months'

LADYSMITH, 1899–1900

The two 4.7-inch and four 12-pounders manned by the naval brigade had to husband their ammunition carefully. They were faced by superior firepower but did just enough to suppress the Boer artillery and beat off at least one determined all-day infantry assault. Thirty-three men were lost from the brigade, twenty-seven of them from disease.

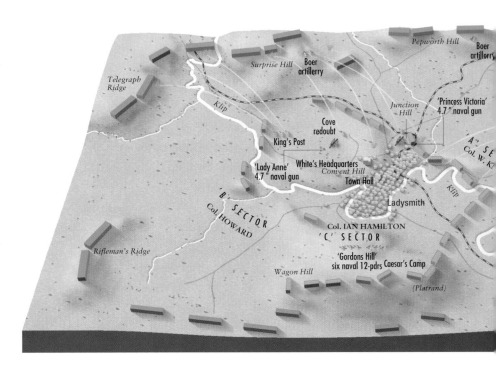

Long Hill

Gun Hill
Boer artillery

Lombard's Kop

'Long Tom'
Mount
Bulwana

hard fighting, in which the naval 4.7-inches and latterly even the famous dismounted 6-inch played a prominent part, that the Tugela River was crossed and the road to Ladysmith was secured. After the relief of Ladysmith the guns of this brigade were gradually handed over to the Royal Artillery.

The third naval brigade joined Lieutenant General Lord Methuen's force moving up the railway line through the Orange Free State towards Kimberley (also under siege) and, eventually, Pretoria. Its composition was similar to that of the other brigades: 400 men and, initially, four 12-pounder guns, though these were later supplemented by 4.7-inch. They were commanded by the gigantic, daunting figure of Captain Prothero ('Prothero the Bad') of the *Doris*.

After her crucial contribution to the initial stages of the Second Boer War, the armoured cruiser Powerful *returns to a warm welcome at Portsmouth in 1900.*

At the battles of Belmont, Graspan and the Modder River the majority of the naval brigade was used as infantry, though the 12-pounders did useful work giving covering fire. Prothero, scorning to take cover, was seriously wounded (though predictably he recovered) and was relieved by Captain Bearcroft of the *Philomel*. Then, in the same week as Colenso ('Black Week'), a British attack at Magersfontein was repulsed with heavy loss. Here the naval guns were misemployed; a preliminary bombardment of the Boer positions was not only ineffective but alerted the defenders to the coming attack.

The arrival of Lord Roberts as Commander-in-Chief, plus considerable further reinforcements from Britain, maintained forward momentum and Kimberley was relieved in February 1900. The naval guns, though still immensely useful, became more and more integrated with the artillery as a whole. An exception was a separate campaign conducted by 'Grant's Guns', two wheeled 4.7-inches manned by an all-naval party of just over fifty, plus the necessary drivers, wagons, horses and trek oxen, which pursued the guerrilla forces of de Wet.

The war dragged on for nearly two more years. The naval brigades' part had been most important in the first three or four months. They provided essential stiffening for the garrison forces, which otherwise might well have been overwhelmed, requiring either British acceptance of Boer control of the whole of South Africa – in the circumstances and spirit of the time, scarcely an option that would have been contemplated – or an amphibious re-entry into the continent which would have been much more costly even than the prolonged and sickly land campaign that actually occurred. The mobility of naval forces, the flexibility of maritime armament and the adaptability of sailors were all well demonstrated.

A 4.7-inch naval gun in action at the battle of Colenso, 15 December 1899. Altogether six such guns, disembarked from ships and hastily adapted, hauled by bullock transport and manned by naval crews, took part in the Second Boer War.

MODDER RIVER AND MAGERSFONTEIN

Naval brigade support throughout Methuen's campaign was mainly in the infantry mode, though 4.7-inch and 12-pounder naval guns were employed. Before the serious reverse at Magersfontein the 4.7-inch naval gun, nicknamed 'Joe Chamberlain', conducted an ill-conceived bombardment of nothing in particular and gave away British intentions.

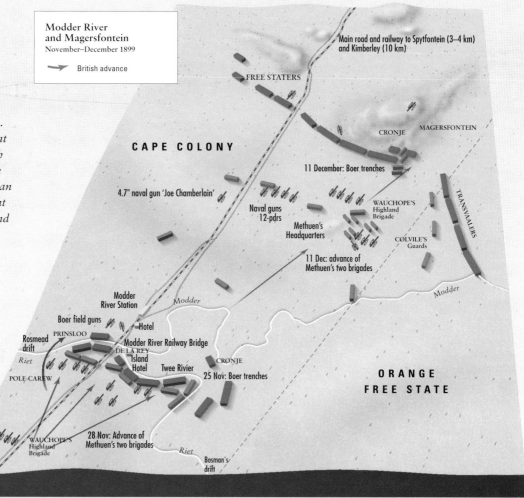

Modder River and Magersfontein
November–December 1899

⟶ British advance

Main road and railway to Spytfontein (3–4 km) and Kimberley (10 km)

FREE STATERS

CAPE COLONY

CRONJE

MAGERSFONTEIN

11 December: Boer trenches

4.7" naval gun 'Joe Chamberlain'

Naval guns 12-pdrs

WAUCHOPE'S Highland Brigade

Methuen's Headquarters

COLVILE'S Guards

TRANSVAALERS

11 Dec: advance of Methuen's two brigades

Modder

Modder

Modder River Station

Boer field guns

Hotel

PRINSLOO

ROSMEAD drift

Modder River Railway Bridge

DE LA REY

Island Hotel

Twee Rivier

CRONJE

ORANGE FREE STATE

Riet

POLE-CAREW

25 Nov: Boer trenches

WAUCHOPE'S Highland Brigade

28 Nov: Advance of Methuen's two brigades

Riet

Bosman's drift

THE BOXER RISING: 1900

Concessions to Western nations in China gave rise once more, in 1900, to rebellion. The Boxers were a society which was passionately anti-foreigner and the Imperial regime was equivocal in its attitude to them. After a succession of 'outrages' against Western interests, British, French, American, Russian and Japanese naval and military forces converged once more on the Peiho and the Taku forts, with the objective of securing the position of Western legations in Peking.

This time the forts were taken without too much difficulty on 16–17 June 1900, assisted by a classical cutting-out operation against four modern Chinese destroyers by the British destroyers *Whiting* and *Fame* (under Lieutenant Roger Keyes). A hiatus followed with the Allied ground forces at bay in Tientsin, but eventually the deadlock was broken and they advanced on Peking, where on 14 August the legations were all relieved. Of the 20,000 or so men employed

HMS Whiting *in Hong Kong, 1900. A destroyer of the China Fleet, she was during the Boxer Rising involved with HMS* Fame *in a classical cutting-out operation on 16–17 June 1900, in which four Chinese destroyers were captured just upstream of the Taku forts.*

ashore, the Japanese contributed nearly half; the British contingent of 3,000 included 1,700 from the Indian Army and a naval brigade of 450, containing as usual a proportion of Royal Marines.

NAVAL BRIGADES IN THE IRONCLAD AGE

Pundits, schooled in the conventions of sea power as they applied in 1905, were inclined to deplore the use of naval personnel in the naval brigade role. The proper employment of sailors, they argued, was in winning battles at sea, and anything that diverted them from that task was misuse. That was an over-simplification derived from command-of-the-sea doctrine. In fact Britain already had that command. She had it absolutely against the adversaries she directly faced throughout this gunboat era, and she had it in sufficient quantity, quality and reputation to deter any intervention against her by other major powers. It was thus open to her to use the sea in any way that was most militarily effective.

CHAPTER SIX

FLEET ACTION

Apotheosis of Commodore Dewey, US Navy. Moving quickly with his Far East Squadron when informed by telegraph of the outbreak of the Spanish–American War, Dewey achieved a crushing victory over Spanish forces in Manila Bay, Philippines, on 1 May 1898 and became an all-American hero.

FLEET ACTION

B Y ONE OF THE SHARPER ironies of the Ironclad Age, which saw the emergence of the doctrine of sea command and the dogma of its achievement by decisive fleet action, there were very few battles between fleets, and of the few that did occur by no means all were decisive. Moreover, as in the American Civil War the lessons were not always readily apparent, nor were they correctly absorbed.

Nevertheless, those half dozen or so battles or campaigns that did occur have their own fascination, and demonstrate if nothing else the problems that confronted the participants in unfamiliar and unforeseen situations, and the limitations imposed by equipments and people untried in battle conditions. That hardly any of these major operations involved the Royal Navy should cause no regret to the historian; the spread of experience adds its own flavour. Some in the Royal Navy at the time sought to learn the lessons; others, perhaps the majority, preferred to bask in their own perceived superiority. A harder schooling was to come.

The earliest European turret-ship to go into action, the Danish Rolf Krake *distinguished herself in the war of 1866 against Prussia and Austria, but was unable to influence the outcome which was decided by Prussian land forces.*

EUROPEAN WARS: 1864–70

The rise of Prussia under Bismarck dominated the decade in Europe. In the fundamentals of the wars that resulted – those against Denmark in 1864, against Austria in 1866 and against France in 1870 – the clash of fleets had little part. They were primarily land wars conducted by a power working from interior lines

of communication, often using the innovation of railways: the essence indeed of the strategies later codified by Sir Halford Mackinder in his counterblast to the theories of Mahan.

But in each there was some maritime element. In 1864, the Prussian assault on Denmark was in danger of being held up by the small but efficient Danish fleet, bolstered by one of the very earliest turret-ships, the *Rolf Krake*, built in Britain and fitted with a Coles turret. The Danes effectively saw off, in the approaches to the Elbe, an Austro-Prussian force under the command of the Austrian Captain W. von Tegetthoff, whom we shall meet again under happier circumstances. But the Danes did not have the resources either to maintain the blockade of the north German ports which they had mounted, or to oppose by sea the Prussian advance into Schleswig, and the war inevitably ended in favour of the more powerful Prussians.

It was a different story, but with a similar outcome, in 1870. The French Navy, incomparably stronger than the Prussian fleet of the time, mounted a blockade of the north German ports and did succeed for a few weeks in inhibiting the trade of great cities like Hamburg. There was no general action; the Prussian Navy did not sally forth and the French did not go in to assault them. Had either occurred, it

The French Navy in the Franco-Prussian War of 1870 mounted a blockade of the Elbe ports but this was ineffective in the face of rapid Prussian victories on land. French heavy ships were of too deep a draught to conduct an assault on the ports themselves.

probably would have ended in a French tactical success but this would have been regarded by Bismarck and von Moltke as a pinprick. They were busy gaining the shattering land victories of Wörth, Gravelotte and Sedan, which swept other considerations aside and comfortably won Germany the war.

The year 1866 was different again. This time the Austrians were ranged against Prussia, and Prussia was in alliance with Italy. Bismarck, capitalizing on the new-found Italian nationalism, held out to the Italians the prize of Venice and in return got a very satisfactory dilution of Austrian force against his own armies. It did not much matter that the Italian army was defeated at Custozza on 24 June; the Prussian victory at Sadowa ten days later was thereby made easier. Negotiations for peace were put in train.

Italian pride however looked for some means of avenging Custozza and, moreover, ensuring that Venice would become part of Italy; and the best instrument was thought to be the Italian fleet, which comfortably outnumbered the Austrian. Count Carlo di Persano, the 60-year-old Commander-in-Chief, was therefore instructed in mid July to take his fleet, then at Ancona, to assault the island of Lissa on the other side of the Adriatic. Lissa was fortified and

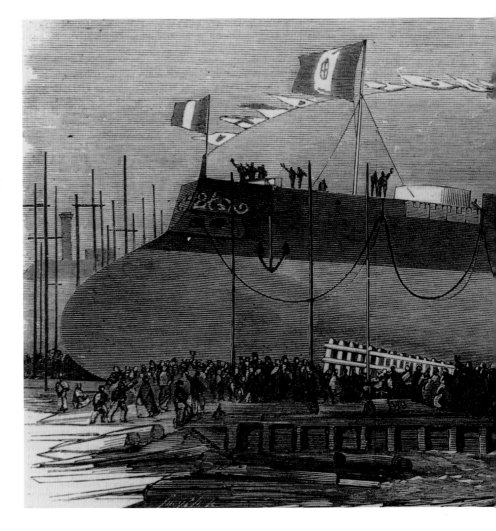

Launch of the Affondatore, *built in Britain for the Italian fleet. Admiral Persano's faith in this ship's speed, manoeuvring and ramming capabilities led him to many tactical errors at Lissa and in the event, presented with the opportunity to ram the Austrian* Kaiser, *he held off.*

mounted eighty-four guns altogether, but the garrison was less than two thousand strong and it was isolated, the Austrian fleet being in Pola, at least a day's steaming away.

Persano's assault on Lissa went slowly, and one of his ships, the ram *Formidabile*, was mauled by the shore batteries and had to retire to Ancona. Even so, when the Austrian fleet under Tegetthoff appeared on the morning of 20 July, the Italians had twelve armoured ships to the Austrians' seven; seventeen unarmoured ships to the Austrians' eleven; and a corresponding preponderance in gun- and manpower. They had moreover the only turret-ship present: the *Affondatore*, built in and newly arrived from Britain, with an exaggerated ram bow that Persano hoped would make her live up to her name, roughly translatable as *Sinker*.

The fleets' states of proficiency, training and leadership told a different story. The Italian Navy was not, in the modern phrase, worked up. Persano had conducted little battle or manoeuvring training and in the assault on Lissa his fleet's activity had been poorly conceived and controlled. His intentions had not been well communicated to his subordinates, and this applied too to the coming

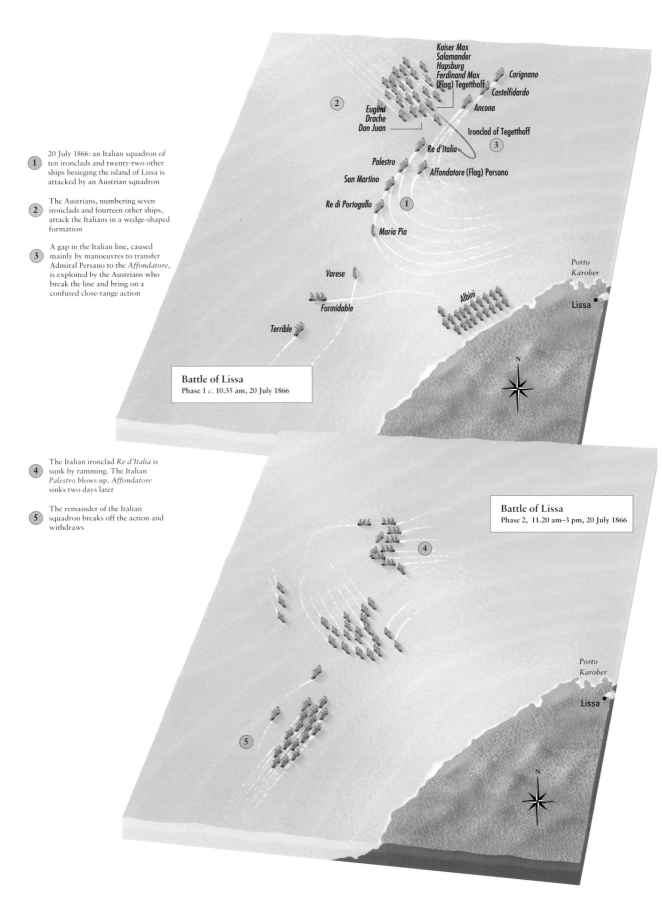

1 20 July 1866: an Italian squadron of ten ironclads and twenty-two other ships besieging the island of Lissa is attacked by an Austrian squadron

2 The Austrians, numbering seven ironclads and fourteen other ships, attack the Italians in a wedge-shaped formation

3 A gap in the Italian line, caused mainly by manoeuvres to transfer Admiral Persano to the *Affondatore*, is exploited by the Austrians who break the line and bring on a confused close-range action

4 The Italian ironclad *Re d'Italia* is sunk by ramming. The Italian *Palestro* blows up. *Affondatore* sinks two days later

5 The remainder of the Italian squadron breaks off the action and withdraws

Kaiser Max
Salamander
Hapsburg
Ferdinand Max
(Flag) Tegetthoff

Carignano
Castelfidardo
Ancona

Eugeni
Drache
Don Juan

Ironclad of Tegetthoff

Re d'Italia

Palestro

Affondatore (Flag) Persano

San Martino

Re di Portogallo

Maria Pia

Varese

Formidable

Albini

Porto
Karober

Lissa

Terrible

Battle of Lissa
Phase 1 *c.* 10.35 am, 20 July 1866

Battle of Lissa
Phase 2, 11.20 am–3 pm, 20 July 1866

Porto
Karober

Lissa

action. The 39-year-old Tegetthoff had been presented with an equally unready fleet, but had done his best to exercise it in the time available and sought to make up for its many shortcomings by fighting spirit and dash, and above all by keeping his plans simple.

This showed in his approach to the battle that followed. Tegetthoff had fully briefed his captains that he intended to lead into action in loose wedge-shaped formation in order to use the ram, and that is just what he did in his flagship the *Ferdinand Max*. His task of disrupting the orthodox line of battle in which the Italians awaited him was enormously helped when Persano, having been guilty of just about every sin of omission of which a fleet commander is capable, now made one of commission too. He left his flagship, the *Re d'Italia*, and embarked in the *Affondatore*, believing no doubt that he could control the action better from there and personally direct this potent vessel to the most critical point. The trouble was that his shift of flag had not been adequately forecast and was not generally known to his fleet, so that his subsequent signals were largely ignored.

Moreover, the *Re d'Italia* had had to stop to make the transfer and this opened up a gap in the Italian line through

LISSA, 20 JULY 1866

The war between Austria and Prussia and Italy had virtually ended in Austria's defeat when Persano, with a large Italian fleet, sought to invade the Dalmatian island of Lissa. The attack next day by a smaller Austrian squadron under Admiral Tegetthoff was notable for ramming tactics. In the confused fighting the Italian battleship Re d'Italia *was rammed and sunk and two other Italian major units lost. Persano's indecision and Tegetthoff's determination were major factors in the outcome. Although both fleets consisted of fully rigged ships, neither used sail at all for battle manouevres.*

LEFT: *Count Carlo Pellion di Persano, who led the Italian fleet. His lack of control of his numerically superior forces was a principal reason for their poor showing.*

which Tegetthoff cheerfully led. The battle then became a mêlée at close range, with the Austrian gunners – serving a far higher proportion of breech-loaders than the Italians – gaining the upper hand and setting fire to one of the smaller Italian ironclads, the *Palestro*. Smoke from this as well as from the guns greatly confused the situation. Vacca, the admiral commanding the Italian van division, made an attempt to double the Austrians; the Italian rear under Albini scarcely came into action at all.

In the murk and confusion the *Re d'Italia* suddenly appeared broadside on ahead of the *Ferdinand Max*. Captain Baron Sterneck in the Austrian flagship ordered full speed and stopped his engine only a cable's length clear of the *Re d'Italia*. The forward momentum of the *Ferdinand Max* carried her ram into the vitals of the Italian ironclad and as she backed off, the *Re d'Italia* heeled over to port and capsized, taking with her two thirds of her crew of 600.

Meanwhile the *Affondatore* had been steaming at high speed hither and thither, seeking without too much conviction for opponents to ram. At one point she was presented with a clear target, the Austrian line-of-battle ship *Kaiser* with a crew of 900, but, for some reason he could not subsequently explain, Persano ordered the *Affondatore* not to proceed. The battle continued to go the Austrians' way; the *Palestro* blew up with heavy loss of life. The Italian fleet retired to Ancona. Tegetthoff, perhaps short of fuel and ammunition, perhaps unwilling to risk his fleet further, did not seek to pursue. Two days later the *Affondatore* foundered in Ancona harbour, *affondato* at last.

Lissa was the most extensive fleet action fought between the start of the Ironclad Age and Tsushima at the end of it, and typifies many of the dilemmas that confronted everyone in these largely experimental fleets, from commanders-in-chief to seamen and stokers. Whether to use gunfire or ram; whether to fight in an orthodox line of battle or a headlong assault designed to bring on a mêlée; how to handle machinery and steering gear, both fragile and vulnerable items (it is notable that neither side dreamed of using sail, though nearly all ships were fully rigged); above all, how to prepare and command fleets in these unfamiliar conditions: all these problems were apparent to those who would study and profit by them. One lesson at least was learnt by some: the establishment and maintenance of the Aim, the cardinal rule of operational planning, was demonstrated by Tegetthoff, and his simple and direct instructions and approach paid handsome dividends.

Strategically, the Austrian victory had almost no effect. In spite of the fire and smoke, the heavy casualties and the sinkings, Lissa was a gesture battle. It may

have exercised some very slight leverage on the final peace settlement but that is hard to discern. The crew of the *Re d'Italia* had shouted and cheered, as she went down, *Venezia e nostra* – 'Venice is ours'. And so, in the event, it was.

THE GUERRA DEL PACIFICO: 1879–83

By the middle of the nineteenth century the whole of South America was free from its former colonial masters. But the young republics were raw and turbulent, eager to exploit the resources they had and make their way in the world. On and near the Pacific coast the resources of nitrates were particularly valuable, and these were an area of contention between Chile on one side and Peru and Bolivia on the other. The dispute led to war in 1879.

The Chilean Navy was larger and more modern than the Peruvian; Bolivia had no navy. Land communications were poor and the war was to a large extent a struggle for the use of the sea. The Chilean Navy mounted a blockade of the Peruvian port of Iquique, while the Peruvian strategy was to conduct a highly mobile sea campaign while avoiding major battle. So far, the war followed classical lines.

Then, in May 1879, the Peruvians succeeded in drawing off the main Chilean force and descended with their two most powerful vessels on the weak Chilean ships left off Iquique. The sloop *Esmeralda* was rammed at the third attempt by the Peruvian turret-ship *Huascar* and sunk, with the loss of her gallant Captain

The Peruvian turret-ship Huascar. *After her brush with the British as a rebel ship in 1877 (see p. 150), she was heavily involved in the Guerra del Pacifico. She had success against inferior forces and as a commerce-raider, but was captured by stronger Chilean units off Angamos Point in October 1879.*

ANGAMOS POINT,
8 OCTOBER 1879

The turret-ship Huascar *was the only remaining major unit of the Peruvian Navy, and the newly-refitted Chilean centre-battery ironclads* Blanco Encalada *and* Cochrane *were deployed to intercept her off Antofagasta. She was first sighted by* Blanco Encalada *who pursued her to the north. The* Cochrane, *steaming fast, intercepted from the port bow and engaged,* Blanco Encalada *joining the action on coming up. Attempts to ram were ineffective but the* Huascar, *losing her Captain Grau and many of her crew, was forced to surrender by gunfire.*

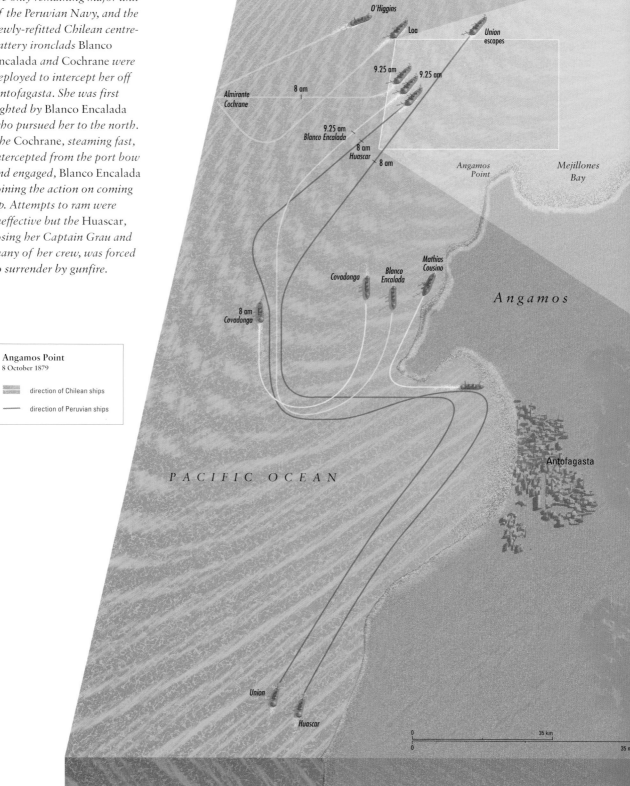

Angamos Point
8 October 1879

direction of Chilean ships

direction of Peruvian ships

O'Higgins

Loa

Union
escapes

9.25 am

9.25 am

Almirante
Cochrane

8 am

9.25 am
Blanco Encalada

8 am
Huascar

8 am

Angamos
Point

Mejillones
Bay

Mathias
Cousino

Covadonga

Blanco
Encalada

Angamos

8 am
Covadonga

Antofagasta

PACIFIC OCEAN

Union

Huascar

0   35 km

0   35 mi

Prat who had attempted single-handedly to board. The Peruvian broadside ironclad *Independencia*, however, paid heavily for her attempt to ram the other Chilean sloop, the *Covadonga*. Venturing too close inshore, she grounded and became a total wreck.

The Peruvians had lost a powerful piece and taken only a pawn. Nevertheless, the *Huascar*, under Admiral Grau, continued to cause a great deal of nuisance, culminating in the capture on 23 July of the Chilean horse-transport *Rimac*. The Chilean Admiral Williams, beset by technical difficulties, lifted the blockade of Iquique and took his main force to Valparaiso to refit; he was there replaced by Commodore Galvarino Riveros. On 20 September the Chilean fleet sailed again, first reinforcing troops at Antofagasta and then splitting into two in the hope of catching the *Huascar*.

On 8 October 1879 that is what happened. The *Huascar* attempted to avoid action, but the newly cleaned Chilean centre-battery ironclads *Cochrane* and *Blanco Encalada* were faster and they brought her to action off Angamos Point at about 9.30 a.m. The contest was unequal, but the *Huascar* fought bravely, suffering many

fatal casualties including Grau himself. She surrendered after an hour and a half's resistance. Nearly all the damage had been done by shellfire from the Chilean muzzle-loaders; several attempts to ram had been ineffective, and indeed one nearly resulted in a 'blue-on-blue' by the *Cochrane* on the *Blanco Encalada*.

The *Huascar* was taken into Chilean service. She had had a curious career; in 1877 she had been taken over by Peruvian rebels during one of their periodic revolutions and had fought an inconclusive action against the British unarmoured cruiser *Shah*. The speed of the *Shah* and the armour of the *Huascar* had cancelled one another out, and the *Shah*'s attack with Whitehead torpedoes – the first ever recorded – was ineffective. The *Huascar* had surrendered to the Peruvian authorities next day, but the *force majeure* had probably been political rather than military. Now she served yet a third master and was a useful adjunct to Chilean forces, which for the rest of the war exercised sea power in a largely classical way, disembarking significant numbers of troops in a series of amphibious operations and helping to end the war in Chile's favour.

ALMIRANTE COCHRANE

Named for Thomas Cochrane, Lord Dundonald, who served the cause of Chilean independence in the 1820s, the Chilean ironclad Almirante Cochrane *was a centre-battery ironclad of classical design. With her sister* Blanco Encalada *she was victorious at the battle of Angamos Point.*

A representation of the battle of Angamos Point. Like many such pictures it represents the information available to the artist at the time. However the perception of very heavy damage to the Huascar *is notable and in accordance with the records.*

The *Guerra del Pacifico* was a truly Mahanian piece in miniature. The attempt by the weaker power to conduct a *guerre de course*; the exercise of the option of blockade by the stronger power; the eventual decisive fleet action; and the subsequent freedom of action conferred by command of the sea: all followed lines that were in course of development by the Colombs and Laughton, and later formed the basis of Mahan's theory. No doubt many in the other hemisphere thought of it as a skirmish by funny foreign fellows in a far-off sea, but some at least held it up as an exemplar and would have been justified in doing so.

THREE EXERCISES IN BRITISH NAVAL SUPREMACY: 1878–85

The Eastern Question, which was the name given to the confused and violent situation that so exercised statesmen in the period from 1875 to 1880, revolved, as so often European turbulence has done, round the Balkans. The Ottoman Empire was in decline; Christian communities were restive; strategic interests were at stake; and no one much trusted anyone else. The principal players were the reforming Czar Alexander II, the Turkish Porte, the Austrian Emperor, and the British Government, who did not always speak with one voice.

It was not, on the face of it, a situation where sea power was likely to have

much influence. Bulgaria was the focus of violence, and though not landlocked was scarcely a place that looked towards the sea. But British strategists, led by Disraeli, could see dangers. They were by now thinking in terms of imperial communications as the arteries and veins of British foreign policy; the Suez Canal had been acquired by Britain in 1875 on that very presumption; Russia was considered to be ambitious and checking her access to the open sea was a prime objective.

Thus, of all the European powers, Britain found herself closer to Turkey than to Russia though she sought to keep clear of war. After several years' fighting and negotiation, matters were thought to have come to a head in January 1878. By then the Turks had suffered many defeats on land at the hands of the Russians, and Britain feared that Russian advances might go unchecked to the Aegean and to Constantinople. Queen Victoria personally intervened with the Czar to ask him to stop.

This was not likely to work unless backed by a show of force, and that was where sea power came in. Admiral Hornby, Commander-in-Chief of the Mediterranean Fleet, which had already exercised a deterrent influence by its presence in Besika Bay, now proceeded with a very powerful force through the Dardanelles. He lay for some weeks in the Sea of Marmora in a high state of readiness, ostensibly to protect the lives of British residents in Constantinople but in reality prepared for sterner battles. Hornby was a highly competent commander, probably the pick of British admirals of the period, and though he was a master of the impressive set piece – of which the

HMS Alexandra, *a potent symbol of British sea power in the 1870s and 1880s. She was one of the most beautiful and comfortable warships afloat, and customarily the flagship of the Mediterranean Fleet. She led the deterrent passage of the Dardanelles in 1878.*

passage of the Dardanelles was a fine example – he would almost certainly have handled his fleet in action well enough to overwhelm any Russian opposition, and of course would either have had support from the Turkish shore works or at least their acquiescence.

He would, moreover, have had ample support from public opinion at home. In the music-halls they sang:

> We don't want to fight, but by jingo, if we do,
> We've got the ships, we've got the men, we've got the money too,
> And the Russians shall not have Constantino ... ple.

Negotiations in the subsequent Congress of Berlin dragged on for months – the Porte had always been stubborn, and now in formal alliance with Britain was no less so – but eventually were concluded on 13 July. Britain could look on the result with satisfaction, for not only had Constantinople been preserved but Bulgaria, clearly a creation of Russia, was to have no access to the Aegean. Coercive deterrence, exercised by sea power, had paid handsomely.

The second exercise of British fleet supremacy also involved the Mediterranean. By 1880 Egypt was in a parlous state and in 1881 a revolt led by Arabi Pasha took a strongly anti-foreigner line and threatened to overturn the rule of the Khedive. Alexandria was its principal power base, and by the end of May 1882 both Britain and France had established a naval presence there. After rioting in the city, foreign nationals were evacuated. Vice Admiral Seymour, now Commander-in-Chief, was much concerned that the shore defences of Alexandria were being reinforced to the extent that they would be able to drive away any force sent against them, and was given permission by the Admiralty to take any action necessary to prevent this. Accordingly he issued an ultimatum to Arabi to expire early on 11 July.

No reply having been received, Seymour put into execution his pre-arranged plan for the bombardment of the

Admiral Sir Geoffrey Phipps Hornby, an outstanding fleet commander of the 1870s. While a master of precise manoeuvres and set-piece displays, he would almost certainly have shown enough flair to cope with any war situation, though his quality was never tested in action.

forts. His force was a very mixed one: eight battleships, mostly centre-battery ironclads with only a few turret-ships and none of the mastless 'Devastation' type, and six smaller craft. Their targeting instructions were precise but they were given latitude as to whether to manoeuvre within their allotted station or to anchor. Fire was to be deliberate and ammunition conserved.

It was a fairly ponderous business, lightened only by the occasional dash of *brio*, for example that of Lord Charles Beresford in the *Condor* who, judging rightly that the Egyptian guns could not fire below a certain depression, took his little vessel close in under Fort Marabout and poured in fire with everything he had, including machine-guns.

Firing continued, at ranges from the forts of between 1,000 and 4,000 yards, until sunset. There was one minor amphibious landing in which a few guns near Mex Fort were spiked. Egyptian return fire was at first hot, but gradually subsided. Casualties and damage in the British fleet were light: five killed and twenty-eight wounded, with all ships battleworthy at the end of the day. When the fleet prepared to resume the assault on the 13th (the weather on the 12th had been too rough for bombardment), it was seen that the works had been abandoned.

However, when landing parties inspected the forts it was found that although the damage inflicted by the 3,000 or so British shells fired looked impressive, in

HMS Alexandra *was not just a pretty flagship: this picture of her centre battery shows the disposition of the heavy guns to enable them to fire over relatively wide angles of bearing.*

fact the majority of the forts' guns could still have been worked. Shock and exhaustion had probably had more effect on the defenders than actual damage. Opinions differed on the accuracy of British fire; Fisher thought it indifferent, while characteristically Percy Scott believed it to have been deplorable.

However stilted the bombardment of Alexandria may have been, it succeeded in its purpose. Arabi Pasha was driven inland, and though his insurrection persisted and was only eradicated eventually by a land campaign that lasted several months, the opening of Alexandria was a necessary facilitator. The lessons so far as sea warfare was concerned were not entirely clear, and indeed are still disputed. While the forts were strong, they were not as strong as some others around the world; while they were well served, they were not served with the

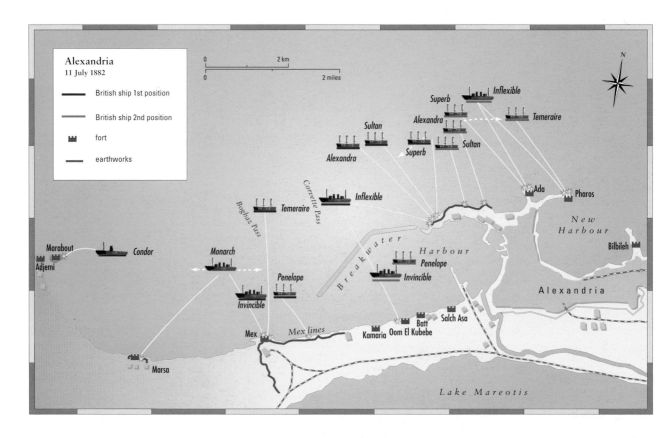

ALEXANDRIA, 11 JULY 1882

The principal action of the powerful British Mediterranean Fleet in the Ironclad Age, the bombardment of Alexandria involved a mixed force of centre-battery and turret-ships, with some gunboats. Based on extensive intelligence, the bombardment was carefully planned and aimed at sequential reduction of the various forts, many of them inadequately constructed and equipped, although their crews responded bravely throughout the day. However the Egyptian defences were abandoned overnight and subsequent landings went largely unopposed.

RIGHT: *An action hero: Lord Charles Beresford as a Rear Admiral. In command of the sloop* Condor *at the bombardment of Alexandria, Beresford took his small vessel close under the guns of an Egyptian fort and laid the foundations of his reputation as a fearless officer.*

tenacity shown by some other defenders in history, before or since. To suggest that Alexandria *proves* that in the late nineteenth century ships could generally defeat forts, without landings to take them in flank or rear, would be going too far in the light of the evidence.

Perceptions count, however, particularly in deterrence, and the third exercise of British power in this period owed a lot to perception. In 1884–5 the 'Great Game' of Russian expansion towards the Indian subcontinent through Afghanistan was in full swing, and in March 1885 Russian forces took an important Afghan position at Pendjeh, threatening further advances. The British response was an example of oblique coercion. Hornby, by now back in Britain, was appointed to head a fleet for the Baltic, specifically directed towards the Russian naval base at Kronstadt. Exercises with an overtly Kronstadt setting were conducted at Berehaven in June, with the Particular Service Squadron, containing all the latest innovations, playing a prominent part. Russia was sensitive to these alarums. She was allowed to retain Pendjeh but her advance was effectively checked.

THE SINO-JAPANESE WAR: 1894–5

Since the opening of the country in the 1860s, Japan had swiftly adapted to Western ways and techniques, not because of any belief in those ways' intrinsic superiority but on the principle that if you could not beat them, you must join them – for the time being at any rate. In the last three decades of the century, therefore, Japan acquired and trained a modern fleet. It was built mostly in European shipyards and armed with European-manufactured weapons; over the years the Imperial Japanese Navy had moved towards a policy of conducting training, apart from some limited technical acquaintance, in Japan.

The process of expansion and modernization was by no means complete when, in 1894, Japan went to war with China. The point of contention was, as so often, Korea: a peninsula so prized and disputed that it might be thought of as a Far Eastern counterpart of Poland. A treaty of 1885 was the latest seeking to govern the tensions between China and Japan, but in the summer of 1894 each country claimed the other had breached it by sending troops to Korea, and war, at first undeclared, broke out – the first shots being fired at sea.

Sea communications were important to both sides. Japan had no land access to Korea, so all her troop movements had to be by water. China did have land access, but roads were bad and railways in that area non-existent. Thus amphibious operations were sure to play a large part in any effective use of military power.

The Chinese Navy was on paper stronger than the Japanese. It had twelve major warships, of which two were properly styled battleships, German-built, each mounting four 12-inch guns and with strong armour. The ten-strong Japanese battle fleet had no similar vessels; although their three largest ships, of French design, mounted 12.6-inch guns, there was only one such gun in each, and

The 'torpedo ram' Polyphemus, *designed to approach and neutralize harbour defences and craft. Though a one-off design, she gained repute as a decisive weapon system and her performance in manoeuvres in 1885 helped to convince Russia that Kronstadt was vulnerable to attack.*

THE YELLOW SEA AREA, 1894–1905

The complexities of the area during this period, with Japanese, Russian and Chinese rivalry over the strategic and resource-rich peninsula of Korea, and the competition for favourable trading bases and conditions amongst the European powers and the USA, are indicated by the map, as well as the principal moves in the Sino-Japanese War.

1. June 1894: Chinese troops arrive to quiet riots at the request of the Korean government
1. Japanese troops arrive (unrequested) to restore order
2. August 1894: Chinese troops sent to northern Korea
2. Japanese troops sent to northern Korea
3. Japanese advance across the Yalu river
4. Japanese land on Liaotung peninsula
5. January 1895: Japanese land on Shantung peninsula and capture Wei-hai-wei
6. February–March 1895: Japanese advance into Manchuria

The Yellow Sea area
1894–1905

Railroad concessions

——— Russian

——— British

——— German

——— French

——— Japanese

——— under Chinese control

Spheres of influence

▨ Russian

▨ British

▨ German

▨ French

▨ Japanese

▨ occupied or ceded to Japan 1895

▨ occupied by Russia 1900

□ leased territory

○ treaty port

● British

● French

○ Japanese

● German

● Portuguese

● US

○ Chinese control

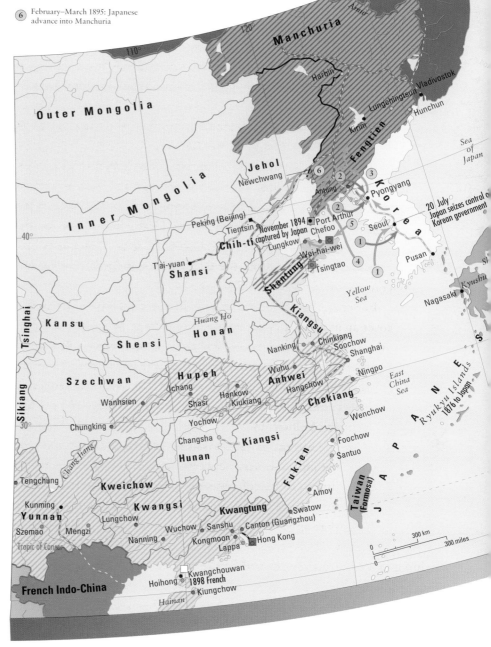

their armour was far weaker than that of the Chinese battleships. They were, by the standards of the day, only cruisers.

However, the events of the war showed that sensible preparation and training could more than make up for numerical and (theoretical) material superiority. Chinese logistics were appalling. Large-calibre ammunition, in particular, was in short supply and what there was showed deficiencies in action; it is said that many shells were filled with cement or sand. Battle training was far inferior to that of the Japanese. Command was patchy; the Chinese Commander-in-Chief, Ting, was personally brave and had ideas as to how to fight a fleet action, but some of his subordinates showed little motivation or professionalism. The Japanese were superior in all these aspects.

The early exchanges of the war involved troop convoy operations by the Chinese and interception by a Japanese 'Flying Squadron' of three cruisers under Admiral Tsuboi, in which the relatively light Chinese escort was overwhelmed, though one Chinese ship escaped to Wei-hai-wei. During subsequent operations against the transports the *Kowshing*, a British steamer on charter to the Chinese and carrying over a thousand Chinese troops, was sunk after repeated warnings by the cruiser *Naniwa*. In command of the *Naniwa* was Captain, later Admiral, Heihachiro Togo: his first appearance on the international scene. No protest was made by Britain, since the flag was not judged to cover such operations on behalf of a belligerent.

In September 1894, the main Chinese fleet was instructed to cover an important troop convoy proceeding towards the mouth of the Yalu River. The disembarkation was successfully achieved, but on 17 September the Japanese fleet appeared from the southward. It was led by Admiral Ito, who had commanded the fleet from the start of the war and had brought it to a high pitch of efficiency.

Ting had no hesitation in offering battle: in any case, the Japanese were between him and his base so there was little chance of evasion. He chose a wedge-shaped formation, reminiscent of Tegetthoff's at Lissa and with what appears to have been the same policy of relying on the ram. However, he was up against a well-organized force fighting in a tight line-ahead, and by the time he reached close range they had already inflicted heavy damage on the Chinese ships, several of which were set on fire. Moreover, when they reached close range they were subjected to the one type of weapon in which the Japanese had undoubted superiority: quick-firing guns. One near-contemporary authority calculated that of guns under

THE YALU, 17 SEPTEMBER 1894

After landing troops in Korea the Chinese force under Admiral Ting was intercepted by a numerically inferior but better-prepared Japanese force under Admiral Ito. The Chinese approached in a wedge formation but against a well-organized Japanese battle line this proved disastrous. The Japanese 'flying squadron' completed the encirclement and the Chinese were lucky to escape with their four remaining heavy units under cover of night.

Admiral Ito, responsible not only for the Japanese success in the battle of the Yalu but for the effective training and preparation of the fleet beforehand.

Ping Yuen
Kwang Ping
Torpedo boats

Yang Wei
ChaoYong
Ching Yuen
Lai Y.
Chen Y.
Ting Y.
King Y.
Chih Y.
KwangKai
Tsi Yuen

3

The battle of the Yalu
17 September 1894

1 17 September 1894: Japanese
   Admiral Ito Yukyo, after landing
   troops to attack the Chinese at
   Pyongyang, sets off to find the
   Chinese squadron commanded by
   Admiral Ting

2 The Japanese squadron consists of
   four heavy cruisers and four light
   fast cruisers plus two old armoured
   cruisers. The main body is in line
   ahead, and a 'flying squadron' of
   fast cruisers is detached to encircle
   the Chinese fleet

3 The Chinese force includes two
   ironclad battleships escorted by four
   light cruisers and six torpedo boats.
   It attacks in a wedge formation
   probably with the intention of
   using the ram as a principal weapon

4 The Japanese squadron, generally
   better handled, outmanoeuvres the
   Chinese, inflicting heavy losses. The
   Japanese fail to destroy the Chinese
   squadron completely but establish
   sea command for the rest of the war

*Admiral Ting, in command
of Chinese forces at the
battle of the Yalu.
Hampered by poor
administration and
undertrained
subordinates, he had
little chance of
success.*

Ping Yuen
Kwang Ping
Torpedo boats

Naniwa
Akitsushima
Takasago
Yoshino
(sunk 2.23 pm)
Saiko

Yang Wei
ChaoYong

Ching Yuen
Lai Y.
Chen Y.
Ting Y.

King Y.
(sunk 3.50 pm)
Chih Y.
(sunk 3.30 pm)
Akagi
Hiyei

Fusoo
Hashidate
Itsuksushima
Chiyoda
Matsushima

4

6-inch calibre but larger than machine-guns, the Japanese mounted sixty-six while the Chinese had only two. This really could produce a 'hail of fire' as the advocates of that theory claimed, and the effect on the remaining effective Chinese ships was devastating.

The battle effectively ended at 5.30 p.m. with four Chinese ships still afloat, under command and mobile, shadowed by Ito with the bulk of his force. He did not intend to risk a night action and expected to finish off the Chinese the next day. They slipped away during the night however, and, with two stragglers joining, six ships – including the two battleships – reached Wei-hai-wei.

The battle of the Yalu was regarded by Western commentators steeped in the doctrine of the decisive battle as only a partial success. It was, for example, learnt afterwards that the Chinese major units were almost completely out of ammunition and could easily have been overwhelmed in the evening of the 17th. There was a general feeling on the other side of the world that 'a determined officer would have done it', and achieved a Nelsonic annihilation.

In fact, however, the Japanese had achieved what they set out to do. Their dominance of the sea for the rest of the war was virtually unchallenged. They were able to *use* the sea (the simple definition and purpose of 'sea power') for transport of troops, and with the help of amphibious forces successively captured the Chinese bases of Port Arthur and Wei-hai-wei, mopping up the Chinese fleet, including the two battleships,

Ting Yuen, built in Germany for China, was the flagship of Admiral Ting in the Sino-Japanese War, 1894–5. *Though sound when built, she suffered from poor maintenance and worse logistical supply.*

in the process. The naval war had not followed an exact Mahanian blueprint, but it was wholly successful.

Technically, there were numerous lessons, not all well learnt. Logistics and quality control are not the most exciting subjects for fighting seamen. The evidence of Chinese unpreparedness was ample, yet as far ahead as the Second, let alone the First, World War there were numerous examples of similar mistakes and omissions, worldwide, in many fields of supply. The danger of fire in action was again demonstrated, and some navies, notably the American, took the lesson (but the Royal Navy's Dunlopillo mattresses did burn fiercely in the Falklands conflict in 1982). Torpedoes were fired on numerous occasions, not only at the Yalu but elsewhere, only the weapons of the smaller craft having any effect; but torpedoes continued to be a part of big ships' armouries till 1945. On one final point, however, there could be little dispute. Training and leadership were shown to be force multipliers. This lesson, at least, was carried into the doctrine of all major navies.

The Japanese cruiser Naniwa, which under the command of Togo Heihachiro carried out the first hostile action of the Sino-Japanese War when after warning she sank a British steamer carrying Chinese troops.

'A Splendid Little War': the Spanish–American Conflict, 1898

By 1898 Mahanian doctrine had spread well beyond the United States of America but they remained its seat: this prophet was respected in his own country. A navalist school now existed in the USA and one of its leaders was Theodore Roosevelt, a Democratic politician who occupied the post of Assistant Secretary of the Navy. Key to his plans for the improvement of the United States' strategic position and influence was the construction of a canal across the Isthmus of Panama. But this in turn entailed securing the strategic position in the Caribbean

A melodramatic rendering of the explosion which destroyed USS Maine *in harbour at Havana, Cuba, on 15 February 1898. Admirals Dewey and Sampson are inset. The Spanish–American War was the inevitable outcome of American outrage.*

so that traffic could pass unhindered through the Canal and on to the eastern seaboard of the USA.

Caribbean stability was endangered, in the view of the navalist school, by turbulence in Cuba. This island, the biggest in the West Indies, was still under Spanish rule but insurrection had been going on for some years. There was much American sympathy for the *insurrectos*. Relations between Spain and the USA became increasingly strained. In January 1898 the American battleship *Maine* was sent to Havana on a 'goodwill visit', generally interpreted as a presence mission to safeguard US nationals. On 15 February she blew up and sank with

RECOVERING THE DEAD BODIES.

Wreckage of the Maine *in Havana harbour. Two separate inquiries were carried out by US investigators and both concluded that Spanish sabotage was responsible, but modern research has cast doubt on these findings.*

great loss of life. Spain was held responsible for the disaster, and two separate US inquiries attributed it to a mine, but the true cause has always been a matter for controversy, observing the number of internal magazine explosions that occurred worldwide during the period 1890–1917 and the fact that Spain had nothing to gain by blowing the *Maine* up.

In any event, war was now inevitable and was formally declared on 24 April. It took the form of a US attack on Spanish interests not only in Cuba but all Spanish possessions. The first in point of time was in the Far East: a tribute to the strategic mobility now given by the telegraph, which could transmit from central government orders that previously would have taken months. Commodore Dewey with the US Asiatic Squadron sailed from Hong Kong waters on 24 April

Commodore Dewey's Far East squadron, in perfect order, entering Manila Bay to defeat the stationed Spanish force. After his inevitable crushing victory, Dewey displayed much diplomacy and American possession of Manila was peacefully achieved.

and by 30 April was off Manila in the Philippines. On 1 May his force of four modern cruisers and two gunboats annihilated a Spanish squadron of about a dozen weak, elderly and poorly maintained vessels lying in the southern part of Manila Bay. Threatened intervention by German forces, pursuing a policy of expansion in the Pacific spurred on by their previous purchase of some other Spanish possessions, came to nothing partly because of British deterrence, and the American flag was finally run up over Manila on 13 August.

Meanwhile, in the Caribbean events were moving rather more slowly. The USA initially hoped to avoid a land campaign in Cuba and to eliminate Spanish power there by a sea blockade combined with supplying the insurrectionists. But this soon began to look too slow a strategy; moreover, a Spanish naval force

The victorious American squadron at the battle of Santiago. As in all such paintings, the ships appear closer together and in better order than they were in real life.

under Admiral Cervera had succeeded in crossing the Atlantic and slipping into the harbour of Santiago on the southern coast of Cuba. Admiral Sampson, the commander of the main American fleet, was reluctant to mount an assault from seaward, since shore defences were thought to be strong and the harbour entrance required intricate navigation. But while Cervera's force was in Santiago public opinion in the USA regarded it as a threat to the whole eastern seaboard.

In consequence, on 22–23 June an American corps was landed 20 miles east of Santiago and advanced slowly towards the town. The Spaniards defended stubbornly but by 1 July Santiago was virtually encircled. General Shafter, the American land commander, was by no means happy with the support he was getting from the navy and he called Sampson to a conference ashore on 3 July.

It was that morning that Cervera, on orders from Madrid, made a dash for it with his force of four armoured cruisers and two destroyers. They did not justify the fears of the American public. They had been sent from Spain, not particularly well-maintained or battle-ready when they departed and in worse condition now.

Admiral William T. Sampson, in charge of the American force off Cuba, 1898. He was ashore, consulting with the land force commander, when the Spanish squadron made its sortie from Santiago and the action was conducted by Commodore Schley.

Admiral Pascual Cervera, the Spanish commander at Santiago. He acted with great courage during the battle, which his weaker squadron had no hope of winning.

Santiago, Cuba, 3 July 1898

The Spanish Admiral Cervera's motley collection of warships was trapped in Santiago, menaced from land by an advancing American force and blockaded by sea. It was ordered by Madrid to attempt to break out, whereupon it was annihilated by a much superior American squadron. This was probably the most one-sided of all the fleet actions of the Ironclad Age.

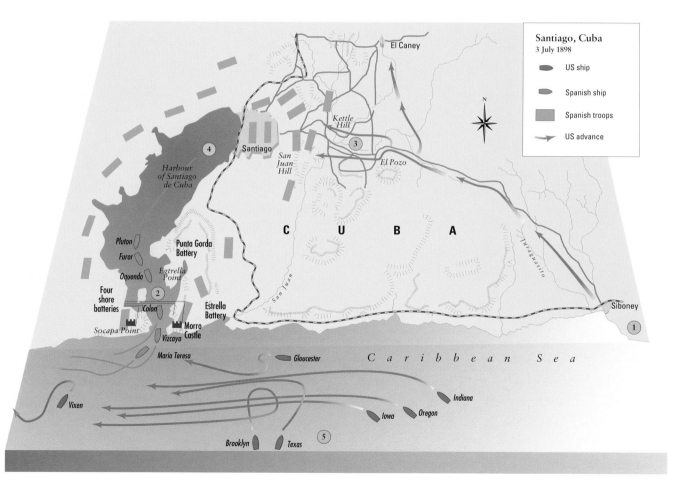

Santiago, Cuba
3 July 1898

- US ship
- Spanish ship
- Spanish troops
- US advance

El Caney

Kettle Hill

Santiago

San Juan Hill

El Pozo

Harbour of Santiago de Cuba

C U B A

Pluton
Furor

Punta Gorda Battery

Oquendo

Estrella Point

Four shore batteries

Colon

Estrella Battery

Socapa Point

Morro Castle

Vizcaya

Maria Teresa

Gloucester

C a r i b b e a n   S e a

Vixen

Indiana

Iowa   Oregon

Brooklyn   Texas

Siboney

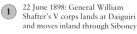
1 22 June 1898: General William Shafter's V corps lands at Daiguiri and moves inland through Siboney

On the night of 2–3 July USS *Merrimac* is sunk to block the harbour entrance

3 1 July: US forces seize San Juan Hill, forcing the Spanish back toward Santiago. The city is now within artillery range of the Americans

4 3 July: Admiral Pascual Cervera is ordered by Madrid to attempt to run the American blockade. The *Maria Teresa* leads the Spanish squadron out past the wreck of the *Merrimac*

5 Commodore Schley, deputizing for Admiral Sampson, immediately gives chase; in under two hours all except one Spanish ship are destroyed. The sole survivor, the *Colón*, is caught some 50 miles west of Santiago when she runs out of fuel

Their supplies were low, coal and ammunition of poor quality. A sense of doom hung about them and it was made no better by the pessimistic (though realistic) predictions of their commander.

Ranged against them was a far superior fleet of four battleships and one heavy cruiser. Their supplies and training were in good order, typified by the extraordinary performance of one of them, the *Oregon*, which since mid April had steamed from the Pacific coast round the Horn in order to reinforce the fleet in the Caribbean. They were under the temporary command of Commodore Schley.

The first report of the Spanish sortie came from the patrolling cruiser *Brooklyn*. The American battleships were ranged in a rough semicircle four miles off the harbour entrance and engaged the Spanish ships in succession as they emerged. Spanish endeavours to maintain a line of battle were disrupted by their own attempts to ram the *Brooklyn*, and the battle quickly became a confused running fight to the westward. The Spanish ships were rapidly hit and set on fire and, one by one, were driven ashore; the furthest any of them got was some 50 miles, achieved by the *Cristobal Colón*, which had she had better quality coal might have escaped entirely. The carnage on board the Spanish ships was severe and they fought with great courage. They were up against an enemy superior in every respect and had no chance. Cervera, who had displayed much personal heroism, survived, was treated with courtesy by his captors and subsequently acquitted by a court martial in Spain.

The war ended in complete success for the United States. Cuba became independent, the Philippines fell under American hegemony and the USA acquired Guam. American eyes were turned outward, Mahan's theories acquired the quality of prophecy, the Panama Canal was built and came under American sway, and Roosevelt eventually became President. Many of these things would have occurred anyway; 'manifest destiny' was already driving the United States onward, but there is no doubt that the beliefs that that destiny lay in the domain of the sea as well as the land, and that a 'navy second to none' was a requirement for the nation, were powerfully reinforced.

THE RUSSO-JAPANESE WAR: 1904–5

While the Sino-Japanese War had ended in Japan's favour, the subsequent Treaty of Shimonoseki had not been so much to her advantage as she could have hoped. The strategically important Liaotung Peninsula, dominating the western approaches to Korea, was to be subject to several foreign concessions; France, Germany and Russia were all to have footholds there, while Britain would occupy Wei-hai-wei. So although Japan co-operated to her advantage with European forces in the Boxer Rising (see Chapter 5), she felt herself constrained in what she regarded as her area of interest.

The Anglo-Japanese Treaty of 1902, whereby Britain guaranteed neutrality in the event of an external Japanese conflict, was of considerable reassurance to

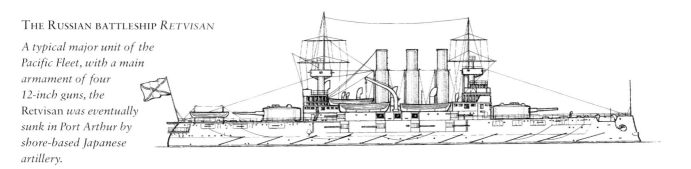

THE RUSSIAN BATTLESHIP *RETVISAN*

A typical major unit of the Pacific Fleet, with a main armament of four 12-inch guns, the Retvisan was eventually sunk in Port Arthur by shore-based Japanese artillery.

The Russian Pacific Fleet flagship Petropavlovsk, *mined in the approaches to Port Arthur, 13 April 1904. Mines accounted for several major warship casualties on both sides in the Russo-Japanese War.*

Japan and encouraged her to try conclusions with Russia, whose occupation of Port Arthur was the chief threat and cause of resentment. Russian annexation of Manchuria in 1903 added to the alarm and by early February 1904 Japan was fully prepared for war.

The Russians thought it unlikely that war would break out, and their central government gave orders that effectively tied the hands of local commanders, including Admirals Alexeiev and Stark in Port Arthur where the main Russian Far East Fleet was assembled. Over 7 and 8 February the situation became increasingly confused and threatening, with Japanese ultimata, troop movements, demonstrations of hostile intent and warnings to neutral warships to get clear, but without a formal declaration of war. No such declaration was made until 10 February.

The first overt Japanese attack took place on Port Arthur over the night of 8–9 February, when three divisions of destroyers, covered by the main fleet under

Admiral Togo, attacked the Russian battleships, whose own patrolling forces were still constrained by their rules of engagement. Altogether some eighteen torpedoes were fired, by far the heaviest torpedo attack ever made up to that time. Two battleships and one cruiser were badly damaged, and the Russian command and fleet were in confusion. Togo did not return with his main fleet off Port Arthur until 11 February, by which time the Russians had recovered somewhat; an exchange of fire by the battleships – by now four effective vessels on either side – and shore batteries was inconclusive. Togo was husbanding his resources, which he rightly believed would be needed for a variety of tasks in the war ahead.

The Russians continued to recover, with a new Commander-in-Chief, Admiral Makarov, a flamboyant character who provided much-needed confidence. The damaged battleships were refloated, a Japanese attempt to use blockships to seal up Port Arthur was frustrated, and sorties increased, menacing Japanese sea communications. On 13 April, however, Russian luck was out. Makarov's flagship, the *Petropavlovsk*, crossed a newly laid Japanese minefield and blew up with great loss of life, including that of the admiral himself. A further mining casualty was the battleship *Pobeida*, which remained afloat though damaged.

Vice Admiral Makarov, Commander-in-Chief of the Russian Pacific Fleet for a few months in 1904. His dynamism could well have been a match for that of Togo himself, but he died when the Petropavlovsk *was mined.*

The Japanese now decided to invest Port Arthur by land, and used their dominance at sea to make the necessary landings. The long campaign that followed was extremely costly to the armies of both sides. Meanwhile, the struggle at sea continued. Admiral Vitgeft assumed command of the Russian fleet and, though not as dynamic as Makarov had been, showed plenty of professional flair and ruthlessness.

On 15 May 1904, the most telling of his initiatives resulted in a black day for the Japanese Navy which almost redressed the balance achieved by their previous successes. The day started badly when, in fog, the heavy cruiser *Kasuga* collided with her consort *Yoshino*. The latter sank almost at once, the former was badly damaged. Later the same day the battleships *Hatsuse* and *Yashima* were mined in a newly laid Russian field, and both sank, the *Hatsuse* with much loss of life.

Encouraged by these Japanese reverses and impelled by the steady encroachment of land forces against the Port Arthur perimeter, Vitgeft made a

sortie in force on 23 June with six battleships, five cruisers and sixteen destroyers. Summoned by wireless reports – this was the first war to use such communications operationally – Togo assembled four battleships, eight cruisers and twenty or more destroyers or torpedo boats. The stage was set for the largest open-sea battle for fifty years. However, when Vitgeft sighted the Japanese fleet it was perfectly placed, lying across his line of advance in excellent order, and he turned for Port Arthur. His ships reached port almost unscathed in spite of fierce night attacks by the Japanese destroyers during which scores of torpedoes were fired.

But the Japanese forces were closing in from landward, and Vitgeft was instructed to seek the relative safety of Vladivostok. He left Port Arthur on 10 August with six battleships, four cruisers and eight destroyers, against which Togo assembled four battleships, four powerful and nine smaller cruisers, and

THE YELLOW SEA, 10 AUGUST 1904

The Russian Pacific Squadron under Admiral Vitgeft made a determined effort to break out of Port Arthur, round the Korean peninsula and make Vladivostok. Intercepted by the Japanese fleet under Togo, they fought an inconclusive running action for several hours. But near nightfall the Japanese scored two crucial hits on the Russian flagship, killing Vitgeft and throwing the Russians into confusion. The Russian main force returned to Port Arthur, some scattered units being interned or defeated in detail.

about forty destroyers and torpedo boats. The Japanese this time had a more numerous and flexible force than the Russians, and provided it was well handled it was likely to prevail.

The opening moves of this battle of the Yellow Sea were complex and skilful on both sides. Gunfire was at long range, often 7,000 yards or more, but fairly accurate; Togo's flagship the *Mikasa* was hit several times. A long running fight to the southward on parallel courses ensued, with little advantage either way, but the Russians were coming ever closer to rounding the southern end of the Korean peninsula and getting away to Vladivostok. Then, at 6.30 p.m. with the light beginning to fail, the fortune of war struck decisively in favour of the Japanese. One shell hit the bridge of Vitgeft's flagship, the *Tzesarevitch*, killing him and most of his staff; another hit her amidships and jammed the helm to port. The Russian fleet fell into confusion, both as to command and to manoeuvre, and the Japanese pounced. The bulk of the Russian heavy ships were gathered by the second-in-command and brought back to Port Arthur, something of a feat in the circumstances; but they had not achieved their aim, and in the ensuing months succumbed to the

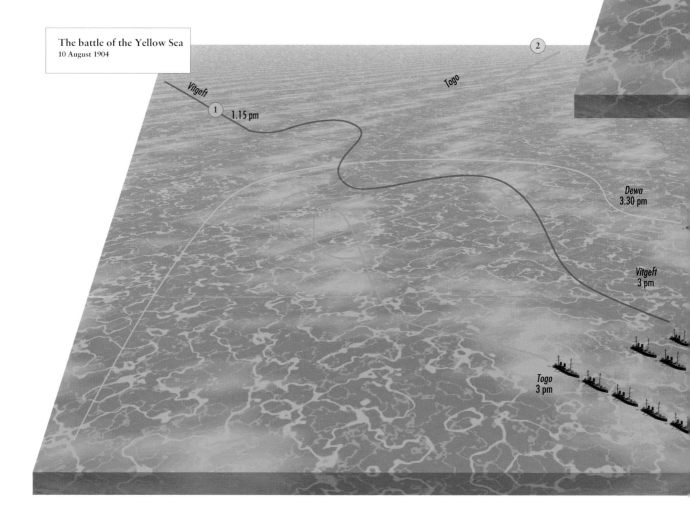

The battle of the Yellow Sea
10 August 1904

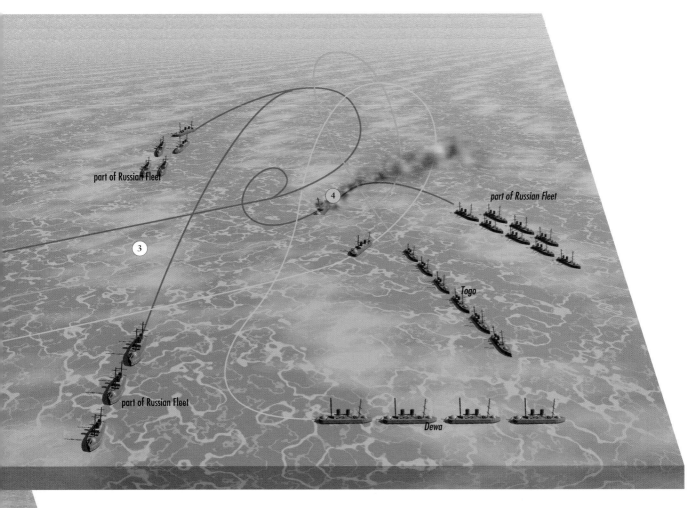

part of Russian Fleet

part of Russian Fleet

③

④

Togo

part of Russian Fleet

Dewa

artillery of the Japanese land forces that were tightening their grip round the base. The *Tzesarevitch* herself reached Kiaochow where she was interned, with some destroyers; the cruiser *Novik* made a run for Vladivostok and was hunted down off Sakhalin.

Meanwhile the Russian cruiser force in Vladivostok, which had harried Japanese sea communications to some effect in the previous three months, sought to support the break-out of the Port Arthur ships. However, they were met on 14 August in the southern Japan Sea by a superior force under Admiral Kamimura, and in the action that followed the 13-year-old Russian cruiser *Rurik* was sunk while the *Rossiya* and *Gromoboi*, both modern and effective ships, suffered severe damage in escaping to Vladivostok.

Thus the Russian naval position in the Far East was, by mid August 1904, almost totally eroded. The Russian high command was faced with the dilemma of either accepting Japanese freedom of action at sea, with all that meant in ability to reinforce the

① 10 August 1904: the Czar orders Admiral Vitgeft to take the Pacific Fleet from Port Arthur to join forces with the Vladivostok squadron

② By midday Admiral Togo closes with the Russian force and opens fire. Dewa's cruisers manoeuvre to contain the Russians

③ Both fleets suffer severe damage after one and a half hours of continuous action

④ At 6.37 pm: two heavy shells hit the *Tzesarevitch* killing Admiral Vitgeft. In the following confusion the Russian fleet scatters and a Russian cruiser is sunk. Most of the Pacific Fleet returns to Port Arthur

mainland at will, or mounting a further challenge. It was decided to do the latter, by what even at the time appeared a desperate throw. This was to send the majority of the Russian Baltic Fleet more than halfway round the world to take on the Japanese Navy. The force sailed on 15 October 1904.

The voyage that followed was an epic. Nothing of the kind had been attempted before, by any navy. The force was a mixed one, composed of some modern ships and some ancient ones. It was led by an Admiral, Rodzhestvensky, of some attainment but uncertain temper, and its officers and men were of varying quality but overall of lower calibre than the already defeated Far East Fleet.

But it was logistics that were the real nightmare. Coal was a constant worry. The total requirement for the whole voyage was half a million tons. A British contractor was engaged and fulfilled his obligations, but the arrangements were extempore and had constantly to be modified. Coal was often carried on upper decks to minimize the frequency of refuelling, but this added to the pervasive dirt and discomfort. Supplies of food and suitable clothing were also hard to come by. Not all ports at which the fleet called were friendly or helpful.

The mood of the fleet was at first excited but brittle, demonstrated by an extraordinary episode in the North Sea when a British fishing fleet was attacked during the night because the Russians believed they were lurking Japanese torpedo boats (Japanese diplomats had not been reluctant to spread rumours that such a threat existed, in spite of its inherent unlikeliness). In the months that followed, gloom took over. A stay of two months at Nossi-Bé, Madagascar, did nothing to restore morale. The fleet was 'reinforced' by a squadron of even more dubious quality under Admiral Nebogatoff, at Cam Ranh Bay in Vietnam in May 1905. By then presentiments of defeat were general.

Nevertheless, Rodzhestvensky forced on. Port Arthur had fallen, there was nothing to reinforce, but a fleet in being in Vladivostok might pose a threat to Japanese communications and perhaps improve any peace settlement. He had some options as to his route, but chose eventually to take the most direct through the Strait of Tsushima, where Togo had expected him to come and had made his dispositions accordingly.

On 27 May the Russians had some reason to hope they had managed to avoid contact in the hazy weather prevailing, but a Japanese auxiliary cruiser sighted them at first light and reported their position to Togo. He was ideally placed and was able to dispose his main force across the Russian line of advance. While the fleets were evenly matched on paper – twelve battleships on each side – the Japanese were fresh, battle-hardened and maintained in good condition, while the Russian ships were foul and in a poor material state, their crews disheartened.

Togo kept it simple. Keeping his battleships in line ahead throughout, he first crossed the Russian 'T' but outside maximum gun range, and then led round in an audacious turn-in-succession which brought his force parallel to the Russians at about 6,000 yards. His flagship did not open fire until this turn was completed.

Admiral Rodzhestvensky, commander of the doomed Baltic Squadron sent by Russia to the Far East in 1904–5. The decisive image in this picture was not borne out by some of his subsequent actions, but his achievement in getting his squadron round the world was remarkable.

The manoeuvre might have been catastrophic against a force with accurate gunnery and fire control, which could have concentrated on the point of turn, but Togo was confident he knew his enemy, and so it proved. Quite apart from anything else, Rodzhestvensky had thrown his own force into confusion by an ill-timed last-minute change in formation.

The outcome was inevitable. Japanese fire was more rapid, more sustained and more accurate. After three quarters of an hour the first of the Russian battleships, the *Osliabia*, sank and several others were in dreadful trouble. Many witnesses afterwards commented on the hail of fire that was now descending on them. The carnage continued; attempts were made by the Russians to preserve order and some sort of line, but one by one the heavy ships were overwhelmed. Rodzhestvensky himself, three times wounded, transferred to a destroyer and the

RUSSIAN BALTIC SQUADRON TO THE FAR EAST, 1904–5

The map shows the coaling points for the three elements of the Russian Baltic Squadron on its epic voyage to defeat at Tsushima. Coal *and other supplies were provided by private contractors and the force often had to anchor well offshore because its presence* *was unwelcome to the coastal authorities. In spite of the organization that went into the passage and its resupply, the expedition was* *doomed as much by weariness and disillusion after its long passage as by its lack of fighting practice and material shortcomings.*

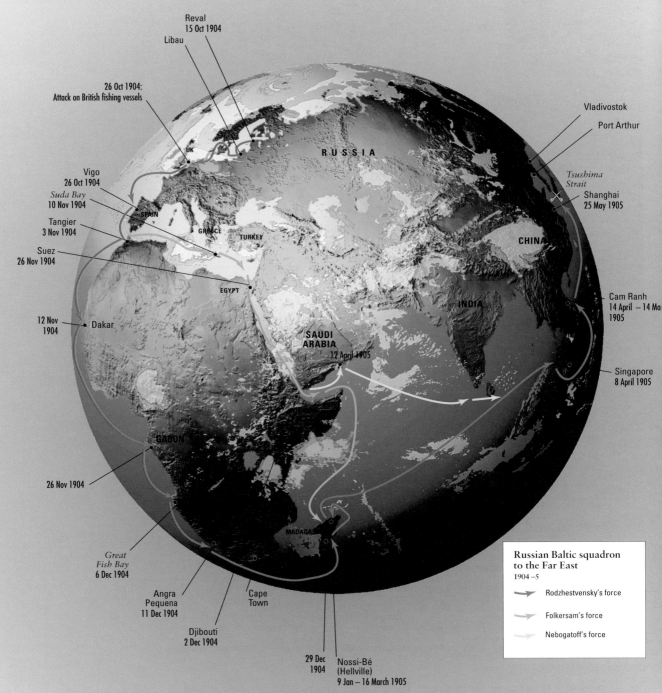

Reval
15 Oct 1904

Libau

26 Oct 1904:
Attack on British fishing vessels

Vigo
26 Oct 1904

Suda Bay
10 Nov 1904

Tangier
3 Nov 1904

Suez
26 Nov 1904

12 Nov
1904 — Dakar

26 Nov 1904

*Great
Fish Bay*
6 Dec 1904

Angra
Pequena
11 Dec 1904

Djibouti
2 Dec 1904

Cape
Town

29 Dec
1904

Nossi-Bé
(Hellville)
9 Jan – 16 March 1905

UK

SPAIN

GREECE

TURKEY

EGYPT

RUSSIA

SAUDI
ARABIA
12 April 1905

INDIA

GABON

MADAGAS

Vladivostok

Port Arthur

*Tsushima
Strait*

Shanghai
25 May 1905

CHINA

Cam Ranh
14 April – 14 Ma
1905

Singapore
8 April 1905

**Russian Baltic squadron
to the Far East**
1904 –5

→ Rodzhestvensky's force

→ Folkersam's force

→ Nebogatoff's force

RUSSO-JAPANESE WAR 1904–5

A general view of the maritime theatre, showing Japanese land advances and the approach route taken by Rodzhestvensky. His other theoretical options, such as rounding the northern tip of Hokkaido, are shown to be so roundabout as to be unrealistic, given his ill-supplied and dispirited squadron.

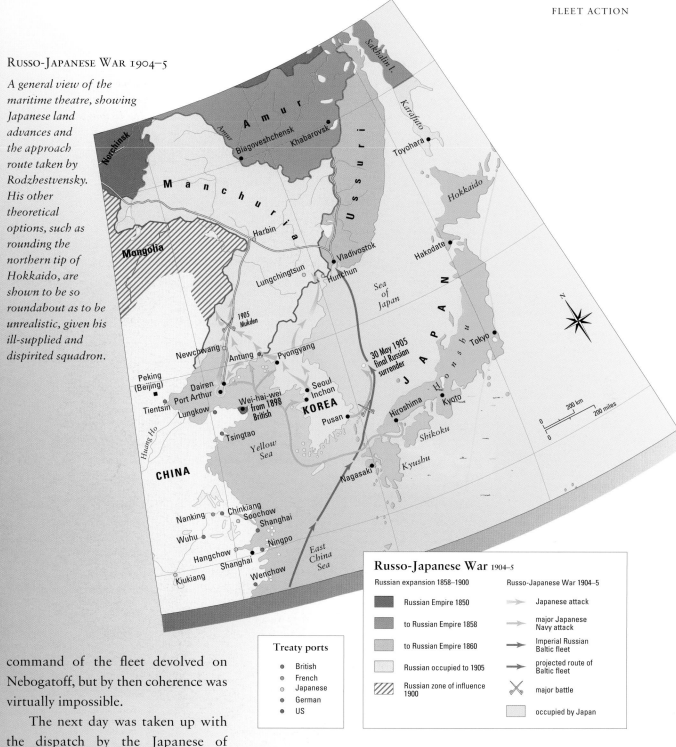

Treaty ports
- British
- French
- Japanese
- German
- US

Russo-Japanese War 1904–5

Russian expansion 1858–1900
- Russian Empire 1850
- to Russian Empire 1858
- to Russian Empire 1860
- Russian occupied to 1905
- Russian zone of influence 1900

Russo-Japanese War 1904–5
- Japanese attack
- major Japanese Navy attack
- Imperial Russian Baltic fleet
- projected route of Baltic fleet
- major battle
- occupied by Japan

command of the fleet devolved on Nebogatoff, but by then coherence was virtually impossible.

The next day was taken up with the dispatch by the Japanese of stragglers from the battle. In all the Russian losses were twelve battleships (of which four surrendered), five cruisers with three more interned in neutral harbours, and six destroyers with one interned. Some 5,000 Russian sailors died and 6,000 were made prisoner.

Tsushima was tactically the most decisive battle of the Ironclad Age. It had been won by a force of superior training and material condition, ably led by a man who above all had correctly assessed his enemy. As such it could be held up by the proponents of what were by now classical theories of sea power, and also by those who were busy elevating the image of Nelson in the Western navies – for Nelson had displayed policies of daring and calculated risk very similar to Togo's.

On analysis, the doctrine of sea command and the dogma of decisive battle are not quite so emphatically proved by Tsushima. It is at least arguable that even had the Russian Squadron won through to Vladivostok, it would have been no more than a nuisance in the strategic situation that then existed, unless it had scored a resounding victory against the Japanese main fleet on the way. That was a most unlikely eventuality, given the morale and material condition of the Russian ships.

Strategically, the battle of the Yellow Sea in August 1904 was more critical than Tsushima. Vitgeft's fleet – battleworthy and based in Vladivostok at that stage of the war – could have been a real menace to Japanese communications. The Japanese achievement in turning it back to Port Arthur ensured that eventually the land-based howitzers would finish it off, and Rodzhestvensky's epic voyage turned into a forlorn hope.

But that is all a matter of hindsight. In the Edwardian summer of 1905, Tsushima was the epitome of sea power. The clash of mighty battle fleets had long been foreseen, the far-reaching effects predicted. Now it had really happened. It was the loudest fanfare of the Ironclad Age. But the *Dreadnought* was laid down in the very same month; Britain already had nearly a dozen submarines; the Wright Brothers had flown in December 1903. The times were about to change with bewildering speed. The Ironclad Age was over.

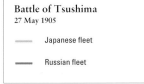

Battle of Tsushima
27 May 1905

Japanese fleet

Russian fleet

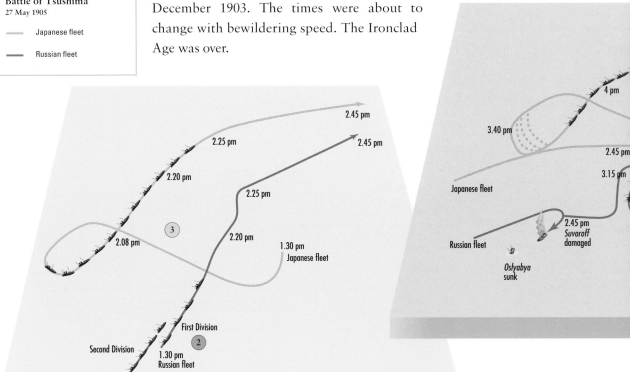

The Russian battleship Osliabia, *typical of the heterogeneous Baltic Squadron and the first casualty of the battle of Tsushima, 27 May 1905.*

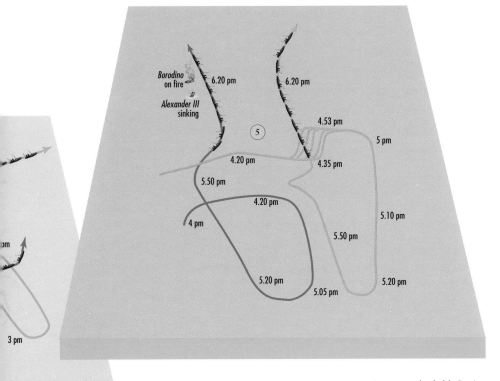

Borodino on fire

Alexander III sinking

6.20 pm
6.20 pm
4.53 pm
5 pm
4.20 pm
4.35 pm
5.50 pm
4.20 pm
5.10 pm
5.50 pm
4 pm
5.20 pm
5.20 pm
5.05 pm
3 pm

TSUSHIMA, 27 MAY 1905

Correctly assessing Russian intentions and warned by efficient reconnaissance, Admiral Togo disposed his main force in an ideal position but crossed the Russian 'T' too far ahead to engage. Meanwhile Rodzhestvensky had put his force into two columns, a poor fighting formation. Togo, now on the Russians' port bow, carried out an audacious turn-in-succession that might have been disastrous against an effective fighting unit. In this case the Japanese emerged unscathed on a parallel course at a good fighting range, and their superior accuracy and rate of fire ensured the almost total destruction of the Russian squadron.

1. 27 May 1905: Admiral Rodzhestvensky enters the Tsushima Straits in line ahead formation, steering north-west. Alerted by an auxiliary merchant cruiser's report, Togo steers to intercept

2. Rodzhestvensky orders an injudicious manoeuvre which put his fleet into two columns, the first division overlapping the other two

3. Togo crosses ahead of the Russian fleet but too far ahead to engage, then carries out a daring turn-in-succession to parallel the Russians' course

4. Japanese manoeuvering, accuracy and rate of fire inflict heavy casualties on the Russian main body

5. Togo utilizing the superior speed of the Japanese ships outmanoeuvres the Russians, sinks and destroys most of the enemy force. Only three Russian ships reach Vladivostok. Three destroyers escape to Manila, the rest are sunk or captured

BIOGRAPHICAL NOTES

AUBE, HYACINTHE-LAURENT-THÉOPHILE (1826–90)
A career naval officer, Aube spent much of his early working life on foreign stations. This probably influenced his naval thought which crystallized in the *Jeune École*, propounding a wartime strategy of ruthless assault on enemy commerce by predominantly light forces, while in peacetime using the same forces for colonial expansion. Aube was Minister of Marine from January 1886 to May 1887 and rapidly turned his theories into plans. The later reversal of these set the French Navy back several years.

BARNABY, SIR NATHANIEL (1829–1915)
A naval architect who entered the service as a draughtsman in Woolwich Dockyard, he was in charge of British naval construction from 1870 to 1885. His span of office included the introduction of turret-ships, the abandonment of sail as the chief motive power of major warships and the selective distribution of armour as a feature of design.

BERESFORD, LORD CHARLES (1846–1919)
A charismatic British naval officer of the old school, Beresford rose to fame in the Egyptian campaigns of 1882 and 1885 as an exponent of gunboat warfare. He was a Member of Parliament sporadically for nearly twenty years and a publicist of navalism. His dispute with Fisher did great harm to the British Navy in the mid 1900s.

BRIN, BENEDETTO (1833–98)
The most famous of Italian ship designers, he specialized in fast, relatively lightly armoured, very heavily gunned, high-freeboard warships, the 'Duilio' and 'Italia' classes being typical. Brin rose in the 1890s to become Minister of the Navy and shares with the French engineer Émile Bertin the unique distinction for a ship designer of having a battleship named after him.

CERVERA Y TOPETE, PASCUAL (1839–1909)
A senior officer of the Spanish Navy in 1898, he led a squadron from Spain to the West Indies to oppose the superior American forces blockading Cuba. He succeeded in getting his ships to Santiago, but his sortie on 3 July (ordered by the government in Madrid) ended predictably in the annihilation of the Spanish force. Cervera was a courageous man but his pessimism was a factor in the Spanish defeat.

COLOMB, SIR JOHN CHARLES READY (1838–1909)
After service in the Royal Marines, he retired at the age of 31 to become a full-time activist on behalf of British naval power. A Member of Parliament for nearly twenty years, he was a prolific pamphleteer, complementing the work of his more historically minded brother, Philip, by relating naval doctrine to contemporary issues.

COLOMB, VICE ADMIRAL PHILIP (1832–99)
A navalist like his brother, he remained a career naval officer for most of his life, retiring in 1886 but becoming an instructor in naval tactics at the Royal Naval College, Greenwich. His authoritarian approach to the subject was reflected in his dedication to elaborate manoeuvres and signalling systems, and his all-or-nothing approach to command of the sea.

CORBETT, SIR JULIAN STAFFORD (1854–1922)
Trained as a barrister, he turned to naval history in the 1890s. From 1895 he published frequently and became a lecturer at the Royal Naval War College, Greenwich in 1902. His doctrines differed significantly from those of Mahan and Colomb in recognizing the limitations of sea power and how it complements land and amphibious operations.

DEWEY, GEORGE (1837–1917)
A career officer in the United States Navy, Dewey

saw extensive action during the Civil War. He introduced modern technology to the US Navy as it began to grow in the late 1880s and 1890s. On the outbreak of the Spanish–American War, in command of the Asiatic Squadron, Dewey moved fast and defeated the Spanish fleet in Manila Bay only a week later. He was subsequently fêted as a hero and held high office for the remainder of his life.

DUPUY DE LÔME, STANILAS CHARLES (1816–85)

A native of Brittany and *Polytechnicien,* he became Director of Material in the French Ministry of Marine in 1858. By then he had already designed the *Napoléon,* said to be the pinnacle of line-of-battle ship design. The *Gloire,* the world's first ironclad, was his greatest achievement, but French technology could not keep up with British as in the *Warrior.* De Lôme then turned to merchant ship construction and was largely responsible for the efficient *Messageries Maritimes* fleet. He also encouraged Gustave Zédé in his submarine ventures.

FARRAGUT, DAVID GLASGOW (1801–70)

Born in the southern state of Tennessee, Farragut served in the war of 1812 against the British. By the outbreak of the Civil War he was a Captain. He took the Union side and was appointed to command the Western Gulf Squadron as Acting Rear Admiral. Subsequent operations against New Orleans and Mobile Bay gave him a reputation for courage and tactical effectiveness, and he was the first man in the US Navy to be accorded the rank of Admiral.

FERRY, JULES (1832–93)

A lawyer by training and journalist by profession before turning to politics, Ferry was twice Prime Minister of France (1880–81, 1883–5). He was active and responsible for change in a great number of fields, including a wholehearted commitment to French colonial expansion, then linked intimately with the French Ministry of Marine. His vision of a chain of bases and coaling stations across the world matched similar British concepts.

FISHER, 'JACKY', JOHN ARBUTHNOT, LORD FISHER OF KILVERSTONE (1841–1920)

In a career ending as an Admiral of the Fleet in the Royal Navy, he distinguished himself in action on several occasions during the Ironclad Age. Dynamic and abrasive, but with compelling charm, he was the moving power behind progress in gunnery, torpedoes, fleet mobility, naval education and training from the middle of the 1870s onwards. His methods outraged more traditional elements of the officer corps, but his overall effect on the Royal Navy was highly beneficial.

HORNBY, SIR GEOFFREY PHIPPS (1825–95)

Hornby joined the Royal Navy at the age of 12, and spent much of his early career on foreign stations. He was a pioneer of 'steam tactics', particularly as Commander-in-Chief in the Mediterranean in 1877–80. He also handled the crisis over the Eastern Question with great skill. A stern but benign disciplinarian, he was much admired and revered in the Service, not least by 'Jacky' Fisher.

ITO YUKYO (1843–1914)

Commander-in-Chief of the Japanese Navy during the Sino-Japanese War, Ito gained a significant victory over the Chinese fleet under Admiral Ting at the Battle of the Yalu in September 1894. He was afterwards criticized for avoiding a dusk action and thereby not completing the annihilation of the Chinese, but their fleet was no longer a serious threat and Japanese command of the sea was assured for the rest of the war.

KNOX LAUGHTON, SIR JOHN (1830–1915)

A graduate of Caius College, Cambridge, Laughton became a naval instructor and after pioneering work in meteorology turned his attention to history, into which, at the Royal Naval Colleges and later at King's College London, he introduced a rigorous research and academic discipline. He founded the Navy Records Society in 1893. His influence on other naval publicists was considerable.

LUCE , STEPHEN BLUCKER (1827–1908)
Entering the US Navy at the age of 14, Luce saw action in the Civil War both as a watch-keeping officer and in command, and later became a proponent of naval education at the highest level. Largely at his urging the Naval War College at Newport, Rhode Island, was founded in 1884 and he became its first President, remaining in office for five years and during this time bringing Alfred T. Mahan into prominence.

MAHAN, ALFRED THAYER (1840–1914)
The most famous theorist of sea power, Mahan was a serving officer in the United States Navy and, as a Captain, was appointed to the US Naval War College in 1886. There he wrote the books, beginning with *The Influence of Sea Power upon History*, which gained worldwide influence in the 1890s. Above all he preached the doctrine of obtaining command of the sea through decisive victory in battle over the main force of the enemy.

MAKAROV, STEPAN OSIPOVICH (1848–1904)
Makarov distinguished himself in the Russo-Turkish War of 1877, conducting torpedo attacks with light craft. He was a pioneer of Arctic exploration. In 1904 he commanded the Russian forces in Port Arthur, and conducted aggressive sorties against the Japanese. He was killed when his flagship the *Petropavlovsk* struck a mine in April 1904. A charismatic, bearded giant, Makarov was a great loss to the Russian Navy.

PERSANO, COUNT CARLO PELLION DI (1806–83)
An officer originally of the Sardinian Navy, Persano came to prominence at the bombardment of Ancona in 1859. He was Navy Minister in the unified Italy of 1862. He was in command of Italian forces at the battle of Lissa in 1866; however, his operational shortcomings and indecision were sadly exposed and his numerically superior force was heavily defeated.

PORTER, DAVID DIXON (1813–91)
Born in Pennsylvania, Porter entered the United States Navy in 1841. In the Civil War he served first under Farragut in the New Orleans campaign, then further up the Mississippi River in the siege and capture of Vicksburg. Towards the end of the war he commanded the final assault on Fort Fisher at the mouth of the Cape Fear River. After the war he was the most prominent figure in US naval administration for many years.

REED, SIR EDWARD JAMES (1830–1906)
A naval architect and Chief Constructor to the British Navy from 1863–70, Reed designed most of the broadside ironclads and the first of the centre-battery ships. After leaving the Admiralty because of technical disputes, he joined the Whitworth organization, remaining active and influential in many fields of maritime development.

RODZHESTVENSKY, ZINOVI PETROVICH (1849–1909)
A gunnery specialist in the Imperial Russian Navy, Rodzhestvensky was a relatively junior admiral when he led the ill-assorted Baltic Squadron halfway round the world to its defeat at Tsushima in 1905. His achievement in getting the ships there at all was remarkable, but on the day his tactical decisions were faulty and only hastened what was probably an inevitable catastrophe.

SAMPSON, WILLIAM THOMAS (1840–1902)
Born in New York, Sampson saw service in the Civil War. Subsequently he filled a number of key posts, including Superintendent of the Naval Academy. In the Spanish–American War of 1898 he commanded the Atlantic Squadron. His dispositions and activity played the major part in the blockade of Cuba and the defeat of the Spanish squadron off Santiago was due largely to his preparations.

SCHLEY, WINFIELD SCOTT (1839–1911)
A native of Maryland, Schley fought on the Union side in the Civil War. His reputation was as a

swashbuckler and risk-taker. In 1898 he was in command of the Flying Squadron as a commodore. In this capacity he won the battle of Santiago, Sampson being temporarily absent on duty. After the battle Schley was court-martialled, mainly for alleged laxity in the preceding months, but also for cowardice during the battle. He was honourably acquitted of the latter charge, but censured on the former.

TEGETTHOFF, WILHELM VON (1827–71)

Born in Styria in the Austro-Hungarian Empire, Tegetthoff progressed through sea and staff appointments to command a squadron off the coast of Denmark in the war of 1864, when his ships came off worse in an encounter with the Danes. He was, however, made Commander-in-Chief of Austrian forces in the Adriatic in 1866, and defeated the Italian fleet at Lissa in August of that year. The battle was notable for the first (and only) use of the ram in open-sea action.

TIRPITZ, ALFRED VON (1849–1930)

Tirpitz entered the Prussian Navy in 1865 and shared the obscurity of that service until the accession of Wilhelm II in 1888. Appointed State Secretary of the Naval Office as a Rear Admiral in 1897, Tirpitz quickly harnessed Wilhelm's enthusiasm and quickly built up the Imperial German Navy as a major force. But it was always a 'risk fleet', designed to threaten the numerically superior Royal Navy with crippling damage and thus to deter Britain from confronting Germany.

TOGO HEIHACHIRO (1846–1934)

A member of the seagoing Satsuma clan, Togo distinguished himself in the Sino-Japanese War of 1894–5 and at the beginning of the Russo-Japanese War was Commander-in-Chief of the Combined Fleet of the Imperial Japanese Navy. His two major victories in that war were at the battle of the Yellow Sea and Tsushima, and his sustained aggression was the principal factor in ensuring Japanese success.

TRYON, SIR GEORGE (1832–93)

Tryon was Executive Officer and Second-in-Command of the *Warrior* in her first commission. This led to many influential appointments. Commander of the Mediterranean Fleet from 1891, Tryon tragically drowned in the *Victoria–Camperdown* collision in June 1893. He was a proponent of rapid battle manoeuvres with minimal signalling, but on this occasion, ironically, the movement was a formal one and either Tryon's intentions were misunderstood or he simply made a mistake.

VITGEFT, VILGELM (1847–1904)

With little reputation in the Russian Navy, Vitgeft commanded the Pacific Fleet after the death of Makarov in April 1904. In August he was ordered to take his fleet to Vladivostok and was encountered by Togo at the battle of the Yellow Sea. Vitgeft's death in this action precipitated a rout and most of the Russian fleet returned to Port Arthur, where it later succumbed to fire from batteries in the surrounding hills.

WHITE, SIR WILLIAM HENRY (1845–1913)

Sometimes called 'the greatest naval architect of all time', White was Director of Naval Construction in Britain from 1886 to 1902. His ships, from the 'Royal Sovereign' through the 'Majestic' to the 'King Edward VII' classes, typify the late Victorian navy – solid, homogeneous, reliable and efficient. White's influence on the Royal Corps of Naval Constructors, formed on his suggestion in 1884, and the Royal Institution of Naval Architects, was immense.

FURTHER READING

In general, secondary sources have been used for this work. Delving into primary documents, many of them in foreign languages because the major actions concerned mainly foreign navies fighting against each other, would be beyond the capacity of most researchers. There is, however, a wealth of contemporary secondary sources that give a flavour of the time, and these are in many cases to be preferred to later accounts.

On *matériel*, the work of David K. Brown, particularly *Warrior to Dreadnought* (Chatham, 1997), has been indispensable. While it perhaps gives more credit to British constructors than some foreign authorities might, it remains of monumental stature. Other authorities on British *matériel* are William Laird Clowes, *The Royal Navy: A History from the Earliest Times to 1900* (republished by Chatham, 1997), vol. VII; Fred T. Jane, *The British Battle Fleet* (first published 1912; republished by Conway, 1997); G. A. Ballard, *The Black Battlefleet* (Nautical Publications Co. and Society for Nautical Research, 1980); and the *Transactions* of the Royal Institution of Naval Architects. Non-British construction was best covered generally by *Conway's All the World's Fighting Ships*, with the work of Theodore Ropp, *The Development of a Modern Navy: French Naval Policy 1871–1904* (Triservice Press, 1987), an essential source concerning France, George Baer's *A Century of Sea Power* (Stanford University Press, 1994) for the USA, Stephen Howarth's *Morning Glory* (Hamish Hamilton, 1983) for Japan, and the work of Holger Herwig, in particular *The German Naval Officer Corps* (Clarendon Press, 1973) and *'Luxury' Fleet* (George Allen and Unwin, 1980) for Germany.

On navies and their people, some of the above authorities were relevant, and more specialized books include John Winton's *Hurrah for the Life of a Sailor!* (London, 1977) and Dennis J. Ringle's *Life in Mr Lincoln's Navy* (US Naval Institute Press, 1998). It was not easy to find accounts of foreign navies specifically in this field, though the work of Ropp, Herwig and Howarth, cited above, filled most of the needs, and a valuable insight into the Russian Navy was given by Richard Hough's *The Fleet that Had to Die* (Hamish Hamilton, 1958). Finally, one must mention here that most important contemporary source, *The Illustrated London News*; though of course British in its slant, it is a most significant chronicle of the time, and the steady rise in the reputation and prestige of navies and sailors – of all nations – during the period is powerfully brought out.

Naval theory is well summarized by Geoffrey Till in *Maritime Strategy and the Nuclear Age* (Macmillan, 2nd edition, 1984) and there are of course many contemporary sources. The works of Alfred Thayer Mahan, particularly *The Influence of Sea Power on Strategy* (Little, Brown, 1892), are well-known, but less so are those of the two Colombs, Corbett (*Some Principles of Sea Power*, 1911) and of the French *Jeune École*, led by Aube. Gerard Noel's *The Gun, Ram and Torpedo* (Griffin, 1874) gives much insight into the difficulties with which tacticians were grappling in that decade, and Andrew Gordon's *The Rules of the Game* (John Murray, 1996) is a modern analysis of command styles.

On the American Civil War, there is a great deal of published material. I have made much use of H. W. Wilson's *Ironclads in Action* (Sampson Low, 1896), Dana M. Wegner in Kenneth J. Hagan (ed.), *In Peace and War* (Greenwood Press, 1978), Raymond Luraghi's *A History of the Confederate Navy* (Chatham, 1996), Charles M. Robinson III's *Hurricane of Fire: The Union Assault on Fort Fisher* (Naval Institute Press, 1998) – which covers a much broader canvas than its title implies – and the Proceedings of the Seventh Franco-British Naval Historical Conference at Brest in 1998, which covered aspects of the Civil War in some detail and have not yet been published.

On navies and imperial expansion, the main sources have been Clowes; Richard Brooks's *The Long Arm of Empire* (Constable, 1999), and the work of Arthur Bleby in *The Naval Review*, both on British naval brigades; Thomas Pakenham's *The Boer War* (Weidenfeld & Nicolson, 1979); and Ropp, on French expansion.

Commentaries on Fleet Actions have made much use not only of Wilson's *Ironclads in Action* but of his later *Battleships in Action* (republished by Conway, 1995). A comprehensive source covering much of the period, and making use of modern research, is Jack Greene and Alessandro Massignani, *Ironclads at War; the Origin and Development of the Armoured Warship, 1854–1891* (Combined Publishing, Pennsylvania, 1998). Other sources were Michel Merys's – *De Lissa à Tsoushima* (Challamel, 1906), *Brassey's Naval Annual*, Hough and Howarth on Tsushima, and for Lissa Clowes's – *Four Modern Naval Campaigns* (Hutchinson, 1906) and Alberto Lumbroso's *La Battaglia di Lissa* (Rivista di Roma, 1910). Sources on the Spanish–American War included Wilson, Baer and Brassey's, noted above, and there is interesting material in James Parker's *Rear Admirals Sampson, Schley and Cervera* (Neale, 1910) and Cervera's own *Spanish Operations in the West Indies* (US Government Printing Office, 1899).

Biographies were put together from various sources, but it must be noted that the Internet is beginning to provide much standard material of this kind – a development probably of more value than the long and indigestible lists of references with which it abounds.

INDEX

PICTURE CREDITS

Every effort has been made to contact the copyright holders for images reproduced in this book. The publishers would welcome any errors or omissions being brought to their attention.

National Maritime Museum, Greenwich: endpaper and pp. 6, 22, 29, 36, 42 (top) 43, 45, 48–9, 51, 52, 53, 56, 57, 61, 62–3, 65, 71, 72, 74–5, 76, 77, 78, 79, 82–3, 90, 95, 98–9, 104, 110–111, 116, 120, 123, 126, 130–31, 132, 147, 148–9, 150–51, 155, 163, 164–5, 166–7, 170, 171, 172–3, 175, 177, 180, 182, 183, 187, 188, 194, 195, 205. Peter Newark's Military Pictures: pp. 14, 18–19, 24, 30, 34, 42 (bottom), 60, 68, 94, 95, 121, 127, 128, 131, 135, 136 (top), 144, 168, 192, 193, 196–7, 198–9, 200, 203, 204, 209, 213. Corbis: pp. 32–3, 80–81, 112 Bettmann, 119 Medford Historical Society Collection, 124, 125 Bettmann, 134, 136 (bottom) 138–9. Mary Evans Picture Library: pp. 38, 39, 160, 184–5. Museo Naval, Madrid: p. 40. Science & Society Picture Library: p. 44. Hulton Getty Picture Collection: pp. 80, 84, 85, 92, 96, 97, 102–3, 153, 201. Royal Naval Museum, Portsmouth pp. 86–7. Bridgeman Art Library: p. 88 Guildhall Art Library, Corporation of London. Bretts, London: p. 108. Reproduced from, Admiral of the Fleet Sir Roger Keyes, *Adventures Ashore and Afloat* (Harrap, 1939): p. 140. Imperial War Museum: p. 145 (Q.69838). Fotomas Index: p. 154. The Art Archive: p. 157. A.K.G.: p. 158–9.

The drawings on pages 48 and 50 are reproduced from *A Short History of Naval and Marine Engineering* by Edgar C. Smith (Cambridge University Press, 1937).

The drawings on the title page and pages 28, 29, 36, 39, 44, 54, 55, 56, 62, 106, 180 and 203 are by Peter Smith and Malcolm Swanston of Arcadia Editions. The drawings on p. 54 are redrawn from drawings from *The Immortal Warrior* by Captain John Wills RN (dec'd) (Kenneth Mason, 1987), and those on p. 106 from drawings in *The Royal Navy: A History from the Earliest Times to 1900* by Sir William Laird Clowes (Sampson Low, Marston and Co., 1903) and *The Rules of the Game* by Andrew Gordon (John Murray, 1996).

ENDPAPER: *Bombardment by Union ironclads and mortar vessels of Island No. 10 in the Mississippi River, March 1862.*